24.95

DATE DUE

MASS VIOLENCE IN AMERICA

MASS VIOLENCE IN AMERICA

THE LOS ANGELES RIOTS

compiled by
Robert M. Fogelson

AYER COMPANY, PUBLISHERS, INC.
SALEM, NEW HAMPSHIRE 03079

Reprint Edition, 1988
Ayer Company, Publishers, Inc.
382 Main Street
Salem, New Hampshire 03079

*

Library of Congress Catalog Card No. 70–90205

*

"White on Black: A Critique of the McCone Commission Report on the Los Angeles Riots" by Robert M. Fogelson is reprinted with permission from the *Political Science Quarterly*, Vol. LXXXII (September, 1967), 337–367.

"The Watts 'Manifesto' and the McCone Report" by Bayard Rustin is reprinted from *Commentary* by permission; Copyright © 1966 by the American Jewish Committee.

"Whitewash Over Watts" by Robert Blauner is reprinted by *Trans*-action by permission; Copyright © 1966 by *Trans*-action magazine, St. Louis, Mo.

*

Manufactured in the United States of America

ISBN 0-405-01311-6

Editorial Note

NATIONS, LIKE MEN, ARE SOMETIMES INTERESTED IN BURYING THE PAST. In early 1968, after more than five years marked by political assassinations, racial uprisings, campus disorders, mass demonstrations and the violent suppression of protest, *The New York Times Magazine* asked a group of distinguished scholars to reply to the question, "Is America by nature a violent society?" In answer, University of Chicago anthropologist Clifford Geertz wrote:

> "We do not know very well what kind of society we live in, what kind of history we have had, what kind of people we are. We are just now beginning to find out, the hard way . . ."

The proposition was astonishing but correct: what was least understood about domestic political violence was its role in American history. It was common knowledge that the United States had had a Revolution, a Civil War, some trouble with the Indians and a period of labor-management conflict. But one could search the shelves of the nation's great libraries without discovering more than a handful of works on the subject of violence in American history, and these hopelessly out of date.

Historians had generally ignored or soft-pedaled the history of farmer uprisings, native vigilantism, labor-management struggles, ethnic conflicts and race riots; comparative work in the history of social conflict was particularly weak. Sociologists and political scientists in the grip of "consensus" theory tended to treat episodes of mass violence in America as insignificant or aberrational—temporary exceptions to the norm of peaceful progress. Psychologists and behavioral scientists discussed "mob violence" in terms which suggested that riots, revolts, insurrections and official violence were the products of individual or group pathology. All such interpretations had the effect not only of minimizing group violence in America, but of depriving it of political content—hence, of relevance to the present.

As a result, as late as 1968, the rich, multifarious and often terrifying history of domestic political violence was still largely *terra incognita*. So long as most Americans wished to keep certain skeletons locked away in their closets, few scholars would attempt to open doors. Conversely, once the American people, frightened yet emboldened by the sudden reappearance of intense social conflict, began to ask new questions about the past, so did the scholars.

Our purpose in helping Arno Press and *The New York Times* select and publish significant documents in the history of political violence has not been to compound past errors by overemphasizing the role of conflict in American history. On the contrary, our aim has been to provide materials which will aid in the search for an accurate perspective on the present. MASS VIOLENCE IN AMERICA includes eyewitness reports, government documents and other descriptive and analytic material relating to mass political violence in the United States. These documents not only provide information—they give the "feel" or "flavor" of past eras of civil disorder by evoking the emotional and political context in which revolts took place. Most of them have long been out of print and are obtainable, if at all, only in the nation's largest libraries.

The scope of this series is wide, ranging from accounts of Indian warfare to descriptions of labor-management violence, from narratives of colonial insurrections to reports on modern racial uprisings. It is not, however, limitless, nor were the constituent volumes carelessly selected. The principle of coherence which guided the selections is implicit in the phrase "mass political violence." "Mass" denotes activity engaged in by large groups rather than individuals acting alone; "political" suggests a relationship between such activity and competition among domestic groups for power, property and prestige; and "violence" is narrowly construed as resulting in physical damage to persons or property. In short, the materials reproduced herein are intended to illuminate the resort to violence by American groups seeking to change or to preserve the status quo. Although historical, they are of interest to any who wishes to understand the causes, nature and direction of domestic political violence, whether they be social scientists, historians or just interested Americans.

Of course, we are particularly hopeful that these volumes will prove useful to those now engaged in curriculum-revision and the teaching of high school and college courses in the area of American studies. What Christopher Jencks and David Reisman term "the Academic Revolution" has made difficult demands on all educators, not the least of which is the demand for courses which are both relevant to the condition of modern America and of the highest academic quality. These volumes are meant to provide raw material for such courses—primary source matter which will help both instructors and students to deepen and enrich their views of the American experience.

Most important, the editors and publisher recognize that these volumes appear during a national crisis which is also a crisis of the spirit, a time in which the public response to various manifestations of civil disorder is increasingly governed by anger, fear and hysteria. In such an atmosphere it is important to recognize that one is not alone in time—that such events have taken place before in America and, unless fundamental changes in our social and political life take place, will probably recur in the future. Our fondest hope is that this work, and others like it, will help to keep alive, in a time of growing unreason, the spirit of reasoned inquiry.

RICHARD E. RUBENSTEIN
The Adlai Stevenson Institute
Chicago, Illinois

ROBERT M. FOGELSON
Harvard-MIT Joint Center
for Urban Studies
Cambridge, Massachusetts

THE LOS ANGELES RIOTS

CONTENTS

I

Page

Violence in the City—An End or a Beginning?
A Report by the Governor's Commission on the
Los Angeles Riots xi

II

White on Black: A Critique of the McCone Commission
Report on the Los Angeles Riots....................................... 111
       ROBERT M. FOGELSON

III

The Watts "Manifesto" and the McCone Report.............. 145
       BAYARD RUSTIN

IV

Whitewash Over Watts: The Failure of the McCone
Commission Report 165
       ROBERT BLAUNER

VIOLENCE IN THE CITY—
AN END OR A BEGINNING?

VIOLENCE IN THE CITY --
AN END OR A BEGINNING?

A REPORT BY THE GOVERNOR'S
COMMISSION ON THE LOS ANGELES RIOTS
December 2, 1965

GOVERNOR'S COMMISSION ON THE LOS ANGELES RIOTS
P.O. BOX 54708, LOS ANGELES, CALIFORNIA 90054

CHAIRMAN
Mr. John A. McCone
VICE CHAIRMAN
Mr. Warren M. Christopher
MEMBERS
Judge Earl C. Broady
Mr. Asa V. Call
The Very Rev. Charles S. Casassa
The Rev. James Edward Jones
Dr. Sherman M. Mellinkoff
Mrs. Robert G. Neumann

December 2, 1965

Dear Governor Brown:

We herewith transmit the report of the Governor's Commission on the Los Angeles Riots.

During the 100 days since you gave us our charge, our Commission has held 64 meetings during which we have received testimony and statements from administrators, law enforcement officers, and others of the State government, of Los Angeles County and city government, and of certain nearby cities also. Additionally, we have received information from representatives of business and labor, and residents of the area where the riots occurred as well as individuals who exercise leadership among these residents. We have heard spokesmen for the Mexican-American minority and social workers and others concerned with minority problems. We have engaged consultants and experts who have reported on particular areas of our concern. In addition, we and our staff have reviewed many reports on Negro problems prepared by government agencies, by universities, and by private institutions.

Transcripts of testimony, depositions, reports of interviews and staff and consultant studies all will be deposited in an appropriate public depository as soon as practicable so that these records can be available to those interested.

Our conclusions and our recommendations are the distillation of the information received from these sources, together with our own observations of existing physical and sociological conditions. We wish to emphasize that, in compliance with your directive, we have been absorbed in the study of the problems in our Negro community. However, we are deeply conscious that the Mexican-American community, which here is almost equal in size to the Negro community, suffers from similar and in some cases more severe handicaps than the Negro

GOVERNOR'S COMMISSION ON THE LOS ANGELES RIOTS
P.O. BOX 54708, LOS ANGELES, CALIFORNIA 90054

CHAIRMAN
Mr. John A. McCone
VICE CHAIRMAN
Mr. Warren M. Christopher
MEMBERS
Judge Earl C. Broady
Mr. Asa V. Call
The Very Rev. Charles S. Casassa
The Rev. James Edward Jones
Dr. Sherman M. Mellinkoff
Mrs. Robert G. Neumann

December 2, 1965
Page 2

community. Also, we are mindful that there are many others within our community living in conditions of poverty and suffering from unemployment and incapacity. In designing programs to assist the Negro, the needs of others must not be overlooked.

We recommend that the Commission reconvene periodically to review actions taken to implement the recommendations in our report, with the next meeting to be held in the summer of 1966.

Respectfully,

John A. McCone, Chairman

Warren M. Christopher, Vice Chairman

Judge Earl S. Broady, Member

Asa V. Call, Member

The Very Rev. Charles S. Cassasa, Member

Reverend James Edward Jones, Member

Dr. Sherman M. Mellinkoff, Member

Mrs. Robert G. Neumann, Member

TABLE OF CONTENTS

Page No.

Letter of Transmittal from the Commission to the Governor
The Governor's Charge to the Commission............................ i
The Crisis — an Overview.. 1
144 Hours in August 1965... 10
Law Enforcement — The Thin Thread............................. 27
Employment — Key to Independence............................... 38
Education — Our Fundamental Resource.......................... 49
The Consumer and the Commuter................................... 62
Welfare and Health.. 69
Neither Slums nor Urban Gems...................................... 75
A Summing Up — The Need for Leadership..................... 81

Appendix
    The Commission Staff.. 89
    Consultants to the Commission... 90
    Clerical and Secretarial Staff.. 92
    List of Sworn Witnesses and other Witnesses...................... 93
    Map of Curfew Area..Inside back cover

CHARGE OF GOVERNOR EDMUND G. BROWN
TO THE COMMISSION
(August 24, 1965)

Chairman McCone and distinguished members of the Commission:

In announcing a week ago that I would appoint a Commission of distinguished Californians to make an objective and dispassionate study of the Los Angeles riots, I emphasized that I would put no limits on the scope of the Commission's inquiries.

Nevertheless, since I was deeply engrossed in this subject almost constantly, day and night, during all of last week, I feel it may be useful if I set out some of the areas in which I hope the Commission will make inquiries and recommendations. In a sense, this is my charge as Governor, to the Commission:

First, I believe that the Commission should prepare an accurate chronology and description of the riots and attempt to draw any lessons which may be learned from a retrospective study of these events. The purpose of this would not be to fix blame or find scapegoats, but rather to develop a comprehensive and detailed chronology and description of the disorders. This should include, by way of example, a study of the following subjects:

A. The circumstances surrounding the arrest which touched off the riots.

B. Why the riots continued and spread, including whether there was any organization, leadership, or outside stimulation of the rioters.

C. The efforts of law enforcement officials to control the riots.

D. The action taken by private individuals, both white and Negro, as well as the leadership in organizations . . . . within or without the troubled area . . . . in attempting to control the riots.

E. Events surrounding the ordering in of the National Guard.

F. The action taken jointly by law enforcement officers and the National Guard to bring the riots under control.

G. The circumstances surrounding the deaths which took place and a consideration of the personal injuries caused.

H. The damage done to property by fires, force, and looting.

I. The weapons used and how they were obtained.

J. The disturbances of a similar nature in other Southern California areas at approximately the same time.

K. The arrests, arraignments and trials of the persons apprehended during the riots.

Second, I believe that the Commission should probe deeply the immediate and underlying causes of the riots. In this connection, the Commission will want to consider the following:

A. The physical and sociological condition in the area of the riots at the time they commenced.

B. The opportunities for Negroes in employment, education, and recreation in the troubled area; and the attitude and awareness of the Negro community regarding those opportunities.

C. The public and private welfare programs available and not available in the area and the extent to which they were utilized.

D. Pertinent facts regarding the persons involved in the riots, including their age, education, job status, habits, family situation, and associations.

E. The attitudes of the rioters toward the community and law enforcement officials in the community and whether these attitudes are supported by fact and reason.

F. The significance of looting in stimulating and prolonging the riots.

Third, the Commission should develop recommendations for action designed to prevent a recurrence of these tragic disorders. The Commission should consider what additional can be done at any level of government or by any agency of the government to prevent a recurrence. Of equal importance, the Commission should consider whether there are steps which private citizens may take, individually or jointly, to prevent a repetition of the bloodshed.

THE CRISIS — AN OVERVIEW

The rioting in Los Angeles in the late, hot summer of 1965 took six days to run its full grievous course. In hindsight, the tinder-igniting incident is seen to have been the arrest of a drunken Negro youth about whose dangerous driving another Negro had complained to the Caucasian motorcycle officer who made the arrest. The arrest occurred under rather ordinary circumstances, near but not in the district known as Watts, at seven o'clock on the evening of 11 August, a Wednesday. The crisis ended in the afternoon of 17 August, a Tuesday, on Governor Brown's order to lift the curfew which had been imposed the Saturday before in an extensive area just south of the heart of the City.

In the ugliest interval, which lasted from Thursday through Saturday, perhaps as many as 10,000 Negroes took to the streets in marauding bands. They looted stores, set fires, beat up white passersby whom they hauled from stopped cars, many of which were turned upside down and burned, exchanged shots with law enforcement officers, and stoned and shot at firemen. The rioters seemed to have been caught up in an insensate rage of destruction. By Friday, the disorder spread to adjoining areas, and ultimately an area covering 46.5 square miles had to be controlled with the aid of military authority before public order was restored.

The entire Negro population of Los Angeles County, about two thirds of whom live in this area, numbers more than 650,000. Observers estimate that only about two per cent were involved in the disorder. Nevertheless, this violent fraction, however minor, has given the face of community relations in Los Angeles a sinister cast.

When the spasm passed, thirty-four persons were dead, and the wounded and hurt numbered 1,032 more. Property damage was about $40,000,000. Arrested for one crime or another were 3,952 persons, women as well as men, including over 500 youths under eighteen. The lawlessness in this one segment of the metropolitan area had terrified the entire county and its 6,000,000 citizens.

Sowing the Wind

In the summer of 1964, Negro communities in seven eastern cities were stricken by riots.* Although in each situation there were unique contributing circumstances not existing elsewhere, the fundamental causes were largely the same:

— Not enough jobs to go around, and within this scarcity not enough by a wide margin of a character which the untrained Negro could fill.

— Not enough schooling designed to meet the special needs of the disadvantaged Negro child, whose environment from infancy onward places him under a serious handicap.

— A resentment, even hatred, of the police, as the symbol of authority.

These riots were each a symptom of a sickness in the center of our cities. In almost every major city, Negroes pressing ever more densely into the central city and occupying areas from which Caucasians have moved in their flight to the suburbs have developed an isolated existence with a feeling of separation from the community as a whole.

---

*   SUMMARY OF 1964 RIOTS

City	Date	Killed	Injured	Arrests	Stores Damaged
New York City	July 18-23	1	144	519	541
Rochester	July 24-25	4	350	976	204
Jersey City	August 2-4	0	46	52	71
Paterson	August 11-13	0	8	65	20
Elizabeth	August 11-13	0	6	18	17
Chicago (Dixmoor)	August 16-17	0	57	80	2
Philadelphia	August 28-30	0	341	774	225

Many have moved to the city only in the last generation and are totally unprepared to meet the conditions of modern city life. At the core of the cities where they cluster, law and order have only tenuous hold; the conditions of life itself are often marginal; idleness leads to despair and finally, mass violence supplies a momentary relief from the malaise.

Why Los Angeles?

In Los Angeles, before the summer's explosion, there was a tendency to believe, and with some reason, that the problems which caused the trouble elsewhere were not acute in this community. A "statistical portrait" drawn in 1964 by the Urban League which rated American cities in terms of ten basic aspects of Negro life — such as housing, employment, income — ranked Los Angeles first among the sixty-eight cities that were examined. ("There is no question about it, this is the best city in the world," a young Negro leader told us with respect to housing for Negroes.)

While the Negro districts of Los Angeles are not urban gems, neither are they slums. Watts, for example, is a community consisting mostly of one and two-story houses, a third of which are owned by the occupants. In the riot area, most streets are wide and usually quite clean; there are trees, parks, and playgrounds. A Negro in Los Angeles has long been able to sit where he wants in a bus or a movie house, to shop where he wishes, to vote, and to use public facilities without discrimination. The opportunity to succeed is probably unequaled in any other major American city.

Yet the riot did happen here, and there are special circumstances here which explain in part why it did. Perhaps the people of Los Angeles should have seen trouble gathering under the surface calm. In the last quarter century, the Negro population here has exploded. While the County's population has trebled, the Negro population has increased almost tenfold from 75,000 in 1940 to 650,000 in 1965.

Much of the increase came through migration from Southern states and many arrived with the anticipation that this dynamic city would somehow spell the end of life's endless problems. To those who have come with high hopes and great expectations and see the success of others so close at hand, failure brings a special measure of frustration and disillusionment. Moreover, the fundamental problems, which are the same here as in the cities which were racked by the 1964 riots, are intensified by what may well be the least adequate network of public transportation in any major city in America.

Looking back, we can also see that there was a series of aggravating events in the twelve months prior to the riots.

— Publicity given to the glowing promise of the Federal poverty program was paralleled by reports of controversy and bickering over the mechanism to handle the program here in Los Angeles, and when the projects did arrive, they did not live up to their press notices.

— Throughout the nation, unpunished violence and disobedience to law were widely reported, and almost daily there were exhortations, here and elsewhere, to take the most extreme and even illegal remedies to right a wide variety of wrongs, real and supposed.

— In addition, many Negroes here felt and were encouraged to feel that they had been affronted by the passage of Proposition 14 — an initiative measure passed by two-thirds of the voters in November 1964 which repealed the Rumford Fair Housing Act and unless modified by the voters or invalidated by the courts will bar any attempt by state or local governments to enact similar laws.

When the rioting came to Los Angeles, it was not a race riot in the usual sense. What happened was an explosion — a formless, quite senseless, all but hopeless violent protest — engaged in by a few but bringing great distress to all.

Nor was the rioting exclusively a projection of the Negro problem. It is part of an American problem which involves Negroes but which equally concerns other disadvantaged groups. In this report, our major conclusions and recommendations regarding the Negro problem in Los Angeles apply with equal force to the Mexican-Americans, a community which is almost equal in size to the Negro community and whose circumstances are similarly disadvantageous and demand equally urgent treatment. That the Mexican-American community did not riot is to its credit; it should not be to its disadvantage.

The Dull Devastating Spiral of Failure

In examining the sickness in the center of our city, what has depressed and stunned us most is the dull, devastating spiral of failure that awaits the average disadvantaged child in the urban core. His home life all too often fails to give him the incentive and the elementary experience with words and ideas which prepares most children for school. Unprepared and unready, he may not learn to read or write at all; and because he shares his problem with 30 or more in the same classroom, even the efforts of the most dedicated teachers are unavailing. Age, not achievement, passes him on to higher grades, but in most cases he is unable to cope with courses in the upper grades because they demand basic skills which he does not possess. ("Try," a teacher said to us, "to teach history to a child who cannot read.")

Frustrated and disillusioned, the child becomes a discipline problem. Often he leaves school, sometimes before the end of junior high school. (About two-thirds of those who enter the three high schools in the center of the curfew area do not graduate.) He slips into the ranks of the permanent jobless, illiterate and untrained, unemployed and unemployable. All the talk about the millions which the government is spending to aid him raise his expectations but the benefits seldom reach him.

Reflecting this spiral of failure, unemployment in the disadvantaged areas runs two to three times the county average, and the employment available is too often intermittent. A family whose breadwinner is chronically out of work is almost invariably a disintegrating family. Crime rates soar and welfare rolls increase, even faster than the population.

This spiral of failure has a most damaging side effect. Because of the low standard of achievement in the schools in the urban core and adjacent areas, parents of the better students from advantaged backgrounds remove them from these schools, either by changing the location of the family home or by sending the children to private school. In turn, the average achievement level of the schools in the disadvantaged area sinks lower and lower. The evidence is that this chain reaction is one of the principal factors in maintaining de facto school segregation in the urban core and producing it in the adjacent areas where the Negro population is expanding. From our study, we are persuaded that there is a reasonable possibility that raising the achievement levels of the disadvantaged Negro child will materially lessen the tendency towards de facto segregation in education, and that this might possibly also make a substantial contribution to ending all de facto segregation.

All Segments of Society

Perhaps for the first time our report will bring into clear focus, for all the citizens to see, the economic and sociological conditions in our city that underlay the gathering anger which impelled the rioters to escalate the routine arrest of a drunken driver into six days of violence. Yet, however powerful their grievances, the rioters had no legal or moral justification for the wounds they inflicted. Many crimes, a great many felonies, were committed. Even more dismaying, as we studied the record, was the large number of brutal exhortations to violence which were uttered by some Negroes. Rather than making proposals, they laid down ultimatums with the alternative being violence. All this nullified the admirable efforts of hundreds, if not thousands, both Negro and white, to quiet the situation and restore order.

What can be done to prevent a recurrence of the nightmare of August? It stands to reason that what we and other cities have been doing, costly as it all has been, is not enough. Improving the conditions of Negro life will demand adjustments on a scale unknown to any great society. The programs that we are recommending will be expensive and burdensome. And the burden, along with the expense, will fall on all segments of our society — on the public and private sectors, on industry and labor, on company presidents and hourly employees, and most indispensably, upon the members and leaders of the Negro community. For unless the disadvantaged are resolved to help themselves, whatever else is done by others is bound to fail.

The consequences of inaction, indifference, and inadequacy, we can all be sure now, would be far costlier in the long run than the cost of correction. If the city were to elect to stand aside, the walls of segregation would rise ever higher. The disadvantaged community would become more and more estranged and the risk of violence would rise. The cost of police protection would increase, and yet would never be adequate. Unemployment would climb; welfare costs would mount apace. And the preachers of division and demagoguery would have a matchless opportunity to tear our nation asunder.

Of Fundamental and Durable Import

As a Commission, we are seriously concerned that the existing breach, if allowed to persist, could in time split our society irretrievably. So serious and so explosive is the situation that, unless it is checked, the

August riots may seem by comparison to be only a curtain-raiser for what could blow up one day in the future.

Our recommendations will concern many areas where improvement can be made but three we consider to be of highest priority and greatest importance.

1. Because idleness brings a harvest of distressing problems, employment for those in the Negro community who are unemployed and able to work is a first priority. Our metropolitan area employs upwards of three millions of men and women in industry and in the service trades, and we face a shortage of skilled and semi-skilled workers as our economy expands. We recommend that our robust community take immediate steps to relieve the lack of job opportunity for Negroes by cooperative programs for employment and training, participated in by the Negro community, by governmental agencies, by employers and by organized labor.

2. In education, we recommend a new and costly approach to educating the Negro child who has been deprived of the early training that customarily starts at infancy and who because of early deficiencies advances through school on a basis of age rather than scholastic attainment. What is clearly needed and what we recommend is an emergency program designed to raise the level of scholastic attainment of those who would otherwise fall behind. This requires pre-school education, intensive instruction in small classes, remedial courses and other special treat ment. The cost will be great but until the level of scholastic achievement of the disadvantaged child is raised, we cannot expect to overcome the existing spiral of failure.

3. We recommend that law enforcement agencies place greater emphasis on their responsibilities for crime prevention as an essential element of the law enforcement task, and that they institute improved means for handling citizen complaints and community relationships.

The road to the improvement of the condition of the disadvantaged Negro which lies through education and employment is hard and long, but there is no shorter route. The avenue of violence and lawlessness leads to a dead end. To travel the long and difficult road will require courageous leadership and determined participation by all parts of our community, but no task in our times is more important. Of what shall it avail our nation if we can place a man on the moon but cannot cure the sickness in our cities?

144 HOURS IN AUGUST 1965

The Frye Arrests

On August 11, 1965, California Highway Patrolman Lee W. Minikus, a Caucasian, was riding his motorcycle along 122nd street, just south of the Los Angeles City boundary, when a passing Negro motorist told him he had just seen a car that was being driven recklessly. Minikus gave chase and pulled the car over at 116th and Avalon, in a predominantly Negro neighborhood, near but not in Watts. It was 7:00 p.m.

The driver was Marquette Frye, a 21-year-old Negro, and his older brother, Ronald, 22, was a passenger. Minikus asked Marquette to get out and take the standard Highway Patrol sobriety test. Frye failed the test, and at 7:05 p.m., Minikus told him he was under arrest. He radioed for his motorcycle partner, for a car to take Marquette to jail, and a tow truck to take the car away.

They were two blocks from the Frye home, in an area of two-story apartment buildings and numerous small family residences. Because it was a very warm evening, many of the residents were outside.

Ronald Frye, having been told he could not take the car when Marquette was taken to jail, went to get their mother so that she could claim the car. They returned to the scene about 7:15 p.m. as the second motorcycle patrolman, the patrol car, and tow truck arrived. The original group of 25 to 50 curious spectators had grown to 250 to 300 persons.

Mrs. Frye approached Marquette and scolded him for drinking. Marquette, who until then had been peaceful and cooperative, pushed her away and moved toward the crowd, cursing and shouting at the officers that they would have to kill him to take him to jail. The patrolmen pursued Marquette and he resisted.

The watching crowd became hostile, and one of the patrolmen radioed for more help. Within minutes, three more highway patrolmen arrived. Minikus and his partner were now struggling with both Frye brothers. Mrs. Frye, now belligerent, jumped on the back of one of the officers and ripped his shirt. In an attempt to subdue Marquette, one officer swung at his shoulder with a night stick, missed, and struck him on the forehead, inflicting a minor cut. By 7:23 p.m., all three of the Fryes were under arrest, and other California Highway Patrolmen and, for the first time, Los Angeles police officers had arrived in response to the call for help.

Officers on the scene said there were now more than 1,000 persons in the crowd. About 7:25 p.m., the patrol car with the prisoners, and the tow truck pulling the Frye car, left the scene. At 7:31 p.m., the Fryes arrived at a nearby sheriff's substation.

Undoubtedly the situation at the scene of the arrest was tense. Belligerence and resistance to arrest called for forceful action by the officers. ˉThis brought on hostility from Mrs. Frye and some of the bystanders, which, in turn, caused increased actions by the police. Anger at the scene escalated and, as in all such situations, bitter recriminations from both sides followed.

Considering the undisputed facts, the Commission finds that the arrest of the Fryes was handled efficiently and expeditiously. The sobriety test administered by the California Highway Patrol and its use of a transportation vehicle for the prisoner and a tow truck to remove his car are in accordance with the practices of other law enforcement agencies, including the Los Angeles Police Department.

The Spitting Incident

As the officers were leaving the scene, someone in the crowd spat on one of them. They stopped withdrawing and two highway patrolmen

−11−

went into the crowd and arrested a young Negro woman and a man who was said to have been inciting the crowd to violence when the officers were arresting her. Although the wisdom of stopping the withdrawal to make these arrests has been questioned, the Commission finds no basis for criticizing the judgment of the officers on the scene.

Following these arrests, all officers withdrew at 7:40 p.m. As the last police car left the scene, it was stoned by the now irate mob.

As has happened so frequently in riots in other cities, inflated and distorted rumors concerning the arrests spread quickly to adjacent areas. The young woman arrested for spitting was wearing a barber's smock, and the false rumor spread throughout the area that she was pregnant and had been abused by police. Erroneous reports were also circulated concerning the treatment of the Fryes at the arrest scene.

The crowd did not disperse, but ranged in small groups up and down the street, although never more than a few blocks from the arrest scene. Between 8:15 p.m. and midnight, the mob stoned automobiles, pulled Caucasian motorists out of their cars and beat them, and menaced a police field command post which had been set up in the area. By 1:00 a.m., the outbreak seemed to be under control but, until early morning hours, there were sporadic reports of unruly mobs, vandalism, and rock throwing. Twenty-nine persons were arrested.

A Meeting Misfires

On Thursday morning, there was an uneasy calm, but it was obvious that tensions were still high. A strong expectancy of further trouble kept the atmosphere tense in the judgment of both police and Negro leaders. The actions by many individuals, both Negro and white, during Thursday, as well as at other times, to attempt to control the riots are commendable. We have heard many vivid and impressive accounts of the work of Negro leaders, social workers, probation officers, churchmen, teachers, and businessmen in their attempts to persuade the people to desist from their illegal activities, to stay in their houses and off the street, and to restore order.

However, the meeting called by the Los Angeles County Human Relations Commission, at the request of county officials, for the purpose of lowering the temperature misfired. That meeting was held beginning about 2:00 p.m. in an auditorium at Athens Park, eleven blocks from the scene of the arrest. It brought together every available representative of neighborhood groups and Negro leaders to discuss the problem. Members of the press, television, and radio covered the meeting. Various elected officials participated and members of the Los Angeles Police Department, Sheriff's Office and District Attorney's Office were in attendance as observers.

Several community leaders asked members of the audience to use their influence to persuade area residents to stay home Thursday evening. Even Mrs. Frye spoke and asked the crowd to "help me and others calm this situation down so that we will not have a riot tonight." But one Negro high school youth ran to the microphones and said the rioters would attack adjacent white areas that evening. This inflammatory remark was widely reported on television and radio, and it was seldom balanced by reporting of the many responsible statements made at the meeting. Moreover, it appears that the tone and conduct of the meeting shifted, as the meeting was in progress, from attempted persuasion with regard to the maintenance of law and order to a discussion of the grievances felt by the Negro.

Following the main meeting, certain leaders adjourned to a small meeting where they had discussions with individuals representing youth gangs and decided upon a course of action. They decided to propose that Caucasian officers be withdrawn from the troubled area, and that Negro officers in civilian clothes and unmarked cars be substituted.

Members of this small group then went to see Deputy Chief of Police Roger Murdock at the 77th Street Station, where the proposals were rejected by him at about 7:00 p.m. They envisaged an untested method of handling a serious situation that was rapidly developing. Furthermore, the proposal to use only Negro officers ran counter to the policy of the Police Department, adopted over a period of time at the urging of Negro leaders, to deploy Negro officers throughout the city and not concentrate them in the Negro area. Indeed, when the proposal came the police had no immediate means of determining where the Negro officers on the forces were stationed. At this moment, rioting was breaking out again, and the police felt that their established procedures were the only way to handle what was developing as another night of rioting. Following those procedures, the police decided to set up a perimeter around the center of trouble and keep all crowd activity within that area.

An Alert Is Sounded

About 5:00 p.m. Thursday, after receiving a report on the Athens Park meeting, Police Chief William H. Parker called Lt. Gen. Roderic Hill, the Adjutant General of the California National Guard in Sacramento, and told him that the Guard might be needed. This step was taken pursuant to a procedure instituted by Governor Brown and agreed upon in 1963 and 1964 between the Los Angeles Police Department, the Governor and the Guard. It was an alert that the Guard might be needed.

Pursuant to the agreed-upon procedure, General Hill sent Colonel Robert Quick to Los Angeles to work as liaison officer. He also alerted the commanders of the 40th Armored Division located in Southern California to the possibility of being called. In addition, in the absence of Governor Brown who was in Greece, he called the acting

Governor, Lieutenant Governor Glenn Anderson, in Santa Barbara, and informed him of the Los Angeles situation.

The Emergency Control Center at Police Headquarters — a specially outfitted command post — was opened at 7:30 p.m. on Thursday. That day, one hundred and ninety deputy sheriffs were asked for and assigned. Between 6:45 and 7:15 p.m., crowds at the scene of the trouble of the night before had grown to more than 1,000. Firemen who came into the area to fight fires in three overturned automobiles were shot at and bombarded with rocks. The first fire in a commercial establishment was set only one block from the location of the Frye arrests, and police had to hold back rioters as firemen fought the blaze.

Shortly before midnight, rock-throwing and looting crowds for the first time ranged outside the perimeter. Five hundred police officers, deputy sheriffs and highway patrolmen used various techniques, including fender-to-fender sweeps by police cars, in seeking to disperse the mob. By 4:00 a.m. Friday, the police department felt that the situation was at least for the moment under control. At 5:09 a.m., officers were withdrawn from emergency perimeter control.

During the evening on Thursday, Lt. Gov. Anderson had come to his home in suburban Los Angeles from Santa Barbara. While at his residence, he was informed that there were as many as 8,000 rioters in the streets. About 1:00 a.m. Friday, he talked by phone to John Billett of his staff and with General Hill, and both advised him that police officials felt the situation was nearing control. About 6:45 a.m., at Lt. Gov. Anderson's request, Billet called the Emergency Control Center and was told by Sergeant Jack Eberhardt, the intelligence officer on duty, that "the situation was rather well in hand," and this information was promptly passed on to Anderson. Anderson instructed Billett to keep in touch with him and left Los Angeles at 7:25 a.m.

for a morning meeting of the Finance Committee of the Board of Regents of the University of California in Berkeley, and an afternoon meeting of the full Board.

Friday, the 13th

Around 8:00 a.m., crowds formed again in the vicinity of the Frye arrests and in the adjacent Watts business area, and looting resumed. Before 9:00 a.m., Colonel Quick called General Hill in Sacramento from the Emergency Control Center and told him riot activity was intensifying.

At approximately 9:15 a.m., Mayor Sam Yorty and Chief Parker talked on the telephone, and they decided, at that time, to call the Guard. Following this conversation, Mayor Yorty went to the airport and boarded a 10:05 flight to keep a speaking engagement at the Commonwealth Club in San Francisco. Mayor Yorty told our Commission that "by about 10:00 or so, I have to decide whether I am going to disappoint that audience in San Francisco and maybe make my city look rather ridiculous if the rioting doesn't start again, and the mayor has disappointed that crowd." The Mayor returned to the City at 3:35 p.m.

The riot situation was canvassed in a Los Angeles Police Department staff meeting held at 9:45 a.m. where Colonel Quick, of the California National Guard, was in attendance, along with police officials. At 10:00 a.m., according to Colonel Quick, Chief Parker said, "It looks like we are going to have to call the troops. We will need a thousand men." Colonel Quick has said that Chief Parker did not specifically ask him to get the National Guard. On the other hand, Chief Parker has stated that he told Colonel Quick that he wanted the National Guard and that Quick indicated that he would handle the request.

In any event, at 10:15 a.m., Colonel Quick informed General Hill by telephone that Chief Parker would probably request 1,000 national guardsmen. General Hill advised Colonel Quick to have Chief Parker call the Governor's office in Sacramento. At 10:50 a.m., Parker made the formal request for the National Guard to Winslow Christian, Governor Brown's executive secretary, who was then in Sacramento, and Christian accepted the request.

By mid-morning, a crowd of 3,000 had gathered in the commercial section of Watts and there was general looting in that district as well as in adjacent business areas. By the time the formal request for the Guard had been made, ambulance drivers and firemen were refusing to go into the riot area without an armed escort.

Calling the Guard

At approximately 11:00 a.m., Christian reached Lt. Gov. Anderson by telephone in Berkeley and relayed Chief Parker's request. Lt. Gov. Anderson did not act on the request at that time. We believe that this request from the chief law enforcement officer of the stricken city for the National Guard should have been honored without delay. If the Lieutenant Governor was in doubt about conditions in Los Angeles, he should, in our view, have confirmed Chief Parker's estimate by telephoning National Guard officers in Los Angeles. Although we are mindful that it was natural and prudent for the Lieutenant Governor to be cautious in acting in the absence of Governor Brown, we feel that, in this instance, he hesitated when he should have acted.

Feeling that he wished to consider the matter further, Lt. Gov. Anderson returned to Los Angeles by way of Sacramento. A propeller-driven National Guard plane picked him up at Oakland at 12:20 p.m., and reached McClellan Air Force Base, near Sacramento, at 1:00 p.m. Anderson met with National Guard officers and civilian staff members and received various suggestions, ranging from advice from Guard officers that he commit the Guard immediately to counsel from some civilian staff members that he examine the situation in Los Angeles and meet with Chief Parker before acting. Although Anderson still did not reach a decision to commit the Guard, he agreed with Guard officers that the troops should be assembled in the Armories at 5 p.m., which he had been told by General Hill was the earliest hour that it was feasible to do so. Hill then ordered 2,000 men to be at the armories by that hour. Anderson's plane left Sacramento for Los Angeles at 1:35 p.m. and arrived at 3:35 p.m.

At the time Lt. Gov. Anderson and General Hill were talking in Sacramento, approximately 856 Guardsmen in the 3rd Brigade were in the Long Beach area 12 miles to the south, while enroute from San Diego, outfitted with weapons, to summer camp at Camp Roberts. We feel it reasonable to conclude, especially since this unit was subsequently used in the curfew area, that further escalation of the riots might have been averted if these Guardsmen had been diverted promptly and deployed on station throughout the riot area by early or mid-afternoon Friday.

Friday afternoon, Hale Champion, State Director of Finance, who was in the Governor's office in Los Angeles, reached Governor Brown in Athens. He briefed the Governor on the current riot situation, and Brown said he felt the Guard should be called immediately, that the possibility of a curfew should be explored, and that he was heading home as fast as possible.

Early Friday afternoon, rioters jammed the streets, began systematically to burn two blocks of 103rd Street in Watts, and drove off firemen by sniper fire and by throwing missiles. By late afternoon, gang activity began to spread the disturbance as far as fifty and sixty blocks to the north.

Lieutenant Governor Anderson arrived at the Van Nuys Air National Guard Base at 3:35 p.m. After talking with Hale Champion who urged him to call the Guard, Anderson ordered General Hill to commit the troops. At 4:00 p.m., he announced this decision to the press. At 5:00 p.m., in the Governor's office downtown, he signed the proclamation officially calling the Guard.

By 6:00 p.m., 1,336 National Guard troops were assembled in the armories. These troops were enroute to two staging areas in the rioting area by 7:00 p.m. However, neither the officials of the Los Angeles Police Department nor officers of the Guard deployed any of the troops until shortly after 10:00 p.m. Having in mind these delays, we believe that law enforcement agencies and the National Guard should develop contingency plans so that in future situations of emergency, there will be a better method at hand to assure the early commitment of the National Guard and the rapid deployment of the troops.

The first death occurred between 6:00 and 7:00 p.m. Friday, when a Negro bystander, trapped on the street between police and rioters, was shot and killed during an exchange of gunfire.

The Worst Night

Friday was the worst night. The riot moved out of the Watts area and burning and looting spread over wide areas of Southeast Los Angeles several miles apart. At 1:00 a.m. Saturday, there were 100 engine companies fighting fires in the area. Snipers shot at firemen as they fought new fires. That night, a fireman was crushed and killed on the fire line by a falling wall, and a deputy sheriff was killed when another sheriff's shotgun was discharged in a struggle with rioters.

Friday night, the law enforcement officials tried a different tactic. Police officers made sweeps on foot, moving en masse along streets to control activity and enable firemen to fight fires. By midnight, Friday, another 1,000 National Guard troops were marching shoulder to shoulder clearing the streets. By 3:00 a.m. Saturday, 3,356 guardsmen were on the streets, and the number continued to increase until the full commitment of 13,900 guardsmen was reached by midnight on Saturday. The maximum commitment of the Los Angeles Police Department during the riot period was 934 officers; the maximum for the Sheriff's Office was 719 officers.

Despite the new tactics and added personnel, the area was not under control at any time on Friday night, as major calls of looting, burning, and shooting were reported every two to three minutes. On throughout the morning hours of Saturday and during the long day, the crowds of looters and patterns of burning spread out and increased still further until it became necessary to impose a curfew on the 46.5 square-mile area on Saturday. Lieutenant Governor Anderson appeared on television early Saturday evening to explain the curfew, which made it a crime for any unauthorized persons to be on the streets in the curfew area after 8:00 p.m.

The Beginning of Control

Much of the Saturday burning had been along Central Avenue. Again using sweep tactics, the guardsmen and police were able to clear this area by 3:30 p.m. Guardsmen rode "shotgun" on the fire engines and effectively stopped the sniping and rock throwing at firemen. Saturday evening, road blocks were set up in anticipation of the curfew. The massive show of force was having some effect although there was still riot activity and rumors spread regarding proposed activity in the south central area.

When the curfew started at 8:00 p.m., police and guardsmen were able to deal with the riot area as a whole. Compared with the holocaust of Friday evening, the streets were relatively quiet. The only major exception was the burning of a block of stores on Broadway between 46th and 48th Streets. Snipers again prevented firemen from entering the area, and while the buildings burned, a gun battle ensued between law enforcement officers, the Guard, and the snipers.

During the day Sunday, the curfew area was relatively quiet. Because many markets had been destroyed, food distribution was started by churches, community groups, and government agencies. Governor Brown, who had returned Saturday night, personally toured the area, talking to residents. Major fires were under control but there were new fires and some rekindling of old ones. By Tuesday, Governor Brown was able to lift the curfew and by the following Sunday, only 252 guardsmen remained.

Coordination between the several law enforcement agencies during ᵗhe period of the riot was commendable. When the California Highway Patrol called for help on Wednesday evening, the Los Angeles Police Department responded immediately. When the situation grew critical Thursday evening, the Los Angeles Sheriff's Office committed substantial forces without hesitation. Indeed, the members of all law enforcement agencies — policemen, sheriff's officers, Highway Patrolmen, city Marshalls — and the Fire Departments as well — worked long hours, in harmony and with conspicuous bravery, to quell the disorder. However, the depth and the seriousness of the situation were not accurately appraised in the early stages, and the law enforcement forces committed and engaged in the several efforts to bring the riots under control on Thursday night and all day Friday proved to be inadequate. It required massive force to subdue the riot, as demonstrated by the effectiveness of the Guard when it moved into position late Friday night and worked in coordination with the local law enforcement units.

Other Areas Affected

As the word of the South Los Angeles violence was flashed almost continuously by all news media, the unrest spread. Although outbreaks in other areas were minor by comparison with those in South Central

-21-

Los Angeles, each one held dangerous potential. San Diego, 102 miles away, had three days of rioting and 81 people were arrested. On Friday night, there was rioting in Pasadena, 12 miles from the curfew zone. There, liquor and gun stores were looted and Molotov cocktails and fire bombs were thrown at police cars. Only prompt and skillful handling by the police prevented this situation from getting out of control.

Pacoima, 20 miles north, had scattered rioting, looting, and burning. There was burning in Monrovia, 25 miles east. On Sunday night, after the curfew area was quiet, there was an incident in Long Beach, 12 miles south. About 200 guardsmen and Los Angeles police assisted Long Beach police in containing a dangerous situation which exploded when a policeman was shot when another officer's gun discharged as he was being attacked by rioters. Several fires were set Sunday night in the San Pedro-Wilmington area, 12 miles south.

Was There a Pre-established Plan?

After a thorough examination, the Commission has concluded that there is no reliable evidence of outside leadership or pre-established plans for the rioting. The testimony of law enforcement agencies and their respective intelligence officers supports this conclusion. The Attorney General, the District Attorney, and the Los Angeles police have all reached the conclusion that there is no evidence of a pre-plan or a pre-established central direction of the rioting activities. This finding was submitted to the Grand Jury by the District Attorney.

This is not to say that there was *no* agitation or promotion of the rioting by local groups or gangs which exist in pockets throughout the south central area. The sudden appearance of Molotov cocktails in quantity and the unexplained movement of men in cars through the areas of great destruction support the conclusion that there was organization and planning after the riots commenced. In addition, on that

—22—

tense Thursday, inflammatory handbills suddenly appeared in Watts. But this cannot be identified as a master plan by one group; rather it appears to have been the work of several gangs, with membership of young men ranging in age from 14 to 35 years. All of these activities intensified the rioting and caused it to spread with increased violence from one district to another in the curfew area.

The Grim Statistics

The final statistics are staggering. There were 34 persons killed and 1,032 reported injuries, including 90 Los Angeles police officers, 136 firemen, 10 national guardsmen, 23 persons from other governmental agencies, and 773 civilians. 118 of the injuries resulted from gunshot wounds. Of the 34 killed, one was a fireman, one was a deputy sheriff, and one a Long Beach policeman.

In the weeks following the riots, Coroner's Inquests were held regarding thirty-two of the deaths.* The Coroner's jury ruled that twenty-six of the deaths were justifiable homicide, five were homicidal, and one was accidental. Of those ruled justifiable homicide, the jury found that death was caused in sixteen instances by officers of the Los Angeles Police Department and in seven instances by the National Guard.**

It has been estimated that the loss of property attributable to the riots was over $40 million. More than 600 buildings were damaged by burning and looting. Of this number, more than 200 were totally destroyed by fire. The rioters concentrated primarily on food markets,

---

* The Coroner's Inquest into one of the deaths was cancelled at the request of the deceased's family. There was no inquest into the death of the deputy sheriff because of pending criminal proceedings.

**A legal memorandum analyzing the procedures followed in the inquests, which was prepared at the request of the Commission, has been forwarded to the appropriate public officials for their consideration.

liquor stores, furniture stores, clothing stores, department stores, and pawn shops. Arson arrests numbered 27 and 10 arson complaints were filed, a relatively small number considering that fire department officials say that all of the fires were incendiary in origin. Between 2,000 and 3,000 fire alarms were recorded during the riot, 1,000 of these between 7:00 a.m. on Friday and 7:00 a.m. on Saturday. We note with interest that no residences were deliberately burned, that damage to schools, libraries, churches and public buildings was minimal, and that certain types of business establishments, notably service stations and automobile dealers, were for the most part unharmed.

There were 3,438 adults arrested, 71% for burglary and theft. The number of juveniles arrested was 514, 81% for burglary and theft. Of the adults arrested, 1,232 had never been arrested before; 1,164 had a "minor" criminal record (arrest only or convictions with sentence of 90 days or less); 1,042 with "major" criminal record (convictions with sentence of more than 90 days). Of the juveniles arrested, 257 had never been arrested before; 212 had a "minor" criminal record; 43 had a "major" criminal record. Of the adults arrested, 2,057 were born in 16 southern states whereas the comparable figure for juveniles was 131. Some of the juveniles arrested extensively damaged the top two floors of an auxiliary jail which had been opened on the Saturday of the riots.

Those involved in the administration of justice — judges, prosecutors, defense counsel, and others—merit commendation for the steps they took to cope with the extraordinary responsibility thrust on the judicial system by the riots. By reorganizing calendars and making special assignments, the Los Angeles Superior and Municipal Courts have been able to meet the statutory deadlines for processing the cases of those arrested. Court statistics indicate that by November 26, the following dispositions had been made of the 2278 felony cases filed against adults: 856 were found guilty; 155 were acquitted; 641 were disposed of prior to trial, primarily by dismissal; 626 are awaiting trial. Of the 1133 misdemeanor cases filed, 733 were found guilty, 81 were acquitted, 184 dismissed and 135 are awaiting trial.

The police and Sheriff's Department have long known that many members of gangs, as well as others, in the south central area possessed weapons and knew how to use them. However, the extent to which pawn shops, each one of which possessed an inventory of weapons, were the immediate target of looters, leads to the conclusion that a substantial number of the weapons used were stolen from these shops. During the riots, law enforcement officers recovered 851 weapons. There is no evidence that the rioters made any attempt to steal narcotics from pharmacies in the riot area even though some pharmacies were looted and burned.

Overwhelming as are the grim statistics, the impact of the August rioting on the Los Angeles community has been even greater. The first weeks after the disorders brought a flood tide of charges and recriminations. Although this has now ebbed, the feeling of fear and tension persists, largely unabated, throughout the community. A certain slowness in the rebuilding of the fired structures has symbolized the difficulty in mending relationships in our community which were so severely fractured by the August nightmare.

The Governor charged the Commission to "probe deeply the immediate and underlying causes of the riots." Therefore, the search for causes, both immediate and long-term, has been our primary objective over the past 100 days. We have all recognized our obligation to find, if we can, the seed bed of violence. This search has taken us to the disciplines of psychology, sociology, economics, and political science, as well as to the curfew area itself. We have crossed and re-crossed various fields of knowledge relevant to our endeavor. In doing so, we have drawn on the expertise and experience of people at many levels of government, in California's leading universities, in business and labor organizations here and elsewhere, as well as of private individuals with long experience in the central Los Angeles area.

It would have simplified our task and assisted enormously in the formulation of our conclusions and recommendations if we could have identified a single cause for the disorder. This was not to be. It is our firm conclusion that no single circumstance can be identified as the sole reason for the August riots; the causes and contributing circumstances were many. It is these circumstances that the balance of the report probes. We start with law enforcement.

LAW ENFORCEMENT — THE THIN THREAD

"As the patriots of seventy-six did to the support of the Declaration of Independence, so to the support of the Constitution and laws let every American pledge his life, his property, and his sacred honor — let every man remember that to violate the law is to trample on the blood of his father and to tear the charter of his own children's liberty. Let reverence for the laws . . . become the political religion of the nation; and let the old and the young, the rich and the poor, the grave and the gay of all sexes and tongues and colors and conditions, sacrifice unceasingly upon its altars."

Abraham Lincoln, January 27, 1837

Maintenance of law and order is a prerequisite to the enjoyment of freedom in our society. Law enforcement is a critical responsibility of government, and effective enforcement requires mutual respect and understanding between a law enforcement agency and the residents of the community which it serves.

The Problem — Deep and Serious

The conduct of law enforcement agencies, most particularly the Los Angeles Police Department, has been subject to severe criticism by many Negroes who have appeared before the Commission as witnesses. The bitter criticism we have heard evidences a deep and long-standing schism between a substantial portion of the Negro community and the Police Department. "Police brutality" has been the recurring charge. One witness after another has recounted instances in which, in their opinion, the police have used excessive force or have been disrespectful and abusive in their language or manner.*

---

* The more than seventy cases of alleged police brutality which were submitted to the Commission contributed to our understanding of the depths of the feelings of a segment of the Negro community toward the Police Department. Because our responsibility has been to review the general policy and procedure for handling citizen complaints rather than to review individual cases, we have referred all of the cases to the appropriate and responsible agencies.

On the other hand, the police have explained to us the extent to which the conduct of some Negroes when apprehended has required the use of force in making arrests. Example after example has been recited of arrestees, both men and women, becoming violent, struggling to resist arrest, and thus requiring removal by physical force. Other actions, each provocative to the police and each requiring more than normal action by the police in order to make an arrest or to perform other duties, have been described to us.

Chief of Police Parker appears to be the focal point of the criticism within the Negro community. He is a man distrusted by most Negroes and they carefully analyze for possible anti-Negro meaning almost every action he takes and every statement he makes. Many Negroes feel that he carries a deep hatred of the Negro community. However, Chief Parker's statements to us and collateral evidence such as his record of fairness to Negro officers are inconsistent with his having such an attitude. Despite the depth of the feeling against Chief Parker expressed to us by so many witnesses, he is recognized, even by many of his most vocal critics, as a capable Chief who directs an efficient police force that serves well this entire community.

With respect to the Los Angeles County Sheriff's Department, the situation is somewhat different. Generally speaking, the Negro community does not harbor the same angry feeling toward the Sheriff or his staff as it does toward the Los Angeles police. Nevertheless witnesses recited to us instances of alleged brutality and excessive use of force by deputy sheriffs on duty.

The reasons for the feeling that law enforcement officers are the enemy of the Negro are manifold and it is well to reflect on them before they are accepted. An examination of seven riots in northern cities of the United States in 1964 reveals that each one was started over a police incident, just as the Los Angeles riot started with the arrest of Marquette Frye. In each of the 1964 riots, "police brutality" was an issue, as it was here, and, indeed, as it has been in riots and insurrections elsewhere in the world. The fact that this charge is repeatedly made must not go unnoticed, for there is a real danger that persistent criticism will reduce and perhaps destroy the effectiveness of law enforcement.

Our society is held together by respect for law. A group of officers who represent a tiny fraction of one percent of the population is the thin thread that enforces observance of law by those few who would do otherwise. If police authority is destroyed, if their effectiveness is impaired, and if their determination to use the authority vested in them to preserve a law abiding community is frustrated, all of society will suffer because groups would feel free to disobey the law and inevitably their number would increase. Chaos might easily result. So, while we must examine carefully the claim of police brutality and must see that justice is done to all groups within our society, we must, at the same time, be sure that law enforcement agencies, upon which so much depends, are not rendered impotent.

Solution is Possible — But Action by Both Police and the Negro Community is Essential

Much can be done to correct the existing impressions and to promote an understanding between the police and the Negro community, and this, we believe, is essential in the interest of crime prevention. The steps that have been taken appear to us to be insufficient. Further action is indicated.

Basically, on the one hand, we call for a better understanding by the law enforcement agencies of Negro community attitudes and, on the other hand, a more widespread understanding within the Negro community of the value of the police and the extent to which the law enforcement agencies provide it with security. Although the criminal element among the Negroes is only a small fraction of the Negro population, over half of all crimes of violence committed in the City of Los Angeles are committed by Negroes, and the great majority of the victims of these crimes are Negroes. Thus, the police, in their effort to suppress crime, are doing so to protect the entire community, including the Negro community.

The Board of Police Commissioners — Strengthening is Needed

The Board of Police Commissioners, as the civilian head of the Police Department, has a great responsibility. It is charged with establishing policies for the Department, supervising and managing the Department, and seeing to it that its policies are followed. In discharging its duties, the Board should have a major role in the improvement and maintenance of police-community relationships. In addition, the Board has extensive responsibilities for the issuance and revocation of permits for carrying on a large number of businesses.

The Commission believes that this Board, meeting one afternoon a week, with compensation of the members of the Board at $10.00 per meeting, cannot and does not exercise the control and direction of the Police Department which is prescribed by the City Charter. It is significant to us that the Board and its actions have not been drawn into the recent criticisms of police conduct in the predominantly Negro areas of the city. Almost without exception, the complaints that we have heard have been directed against Chief Parker and the police officers. No one, not a single witness, has criticized the Board for the conduct of the police, although the Board is the final authority in such matters. We interpret this as evidence that the Board of Police Commissioners is not visibly exercising the authority over the Department vested in it by the City Charter. Our own investigation and evaluation, and the testimony of witnesses, confirm this.

Therefore, we urge that steps be taken immediately to arm the Board of Police Commissioners with all necessary tools to discharge its City Charter responsibilities. This will mean increased compensation for the Commissioners, more frequent meetings of the Board, a larger staff, and a revision of procedures that have been followed in the past. A Board, shouldering the responsibilities envisaged here, must be composed of capable and dedicated men, chosen by the Mayor and confirmed by the City Council, willing to devote the necessary time and thoughtful effort to the task.

Complaint Procedures — A New Approach to an Old Problem

A strained relationship such as we have observed as existing between the police and the Negro community can be relieved only if the citizen knows that he will be fairly and properly treated, that his complaints of police misconduct will be heard and investigated, and that, if justified, disciplinary action will be taken against the offending officer.

Under the present Police Department procedure, citizen complaints are received by the Police Department or by the Board of Police Commissioners. All investigations of citizen complaints, wherever received, are conducted under the overall supervision of the Internal Affairs Division of the Police Department. In the vast majority of cases, primary responsibility for investigating allegations of officer misconduct has in the past been placed with the division commander of the individual officer involved. After the investigation has been completed, the determination whether a complaint should be sustained is made either by the Chief of Police or by the Board of Police Commissioners, depending upon where the complaint was originally filed. Where a complaint is sustained, responsibility for discipline is vested in the Chief of Police and the Board of Rights, which provides a departmental hearing to an accused officer before serious sanctions can be imposed.

The Commission has concluded that there are several deficiencies in this existing procedure. We believe that division commanders and those in the command structure should not conduct investigations of complaints with respect to their own subordinate officers. Moreover, existing procedures are not sufficiently visible to or understood by the public. Finally, we do not think there should be a difference, as there now is, in the handling of a complaint depending solely upon whether it was filed with the Board or the Police Department.

Under the existing procedure, the impression is widespread that complaints by civilians go unnoticed, that police officers are free to conduct themselves as they will, and that the manner in which they handle the public is of little concern to the higher authorities. This impression is not consistent with fact. Departmental policies set high standards of conduct for police officers in their contacts with citizens, and these standards are conscientiously enforced. In 1964, 412 complaints of police misconduct were received from citizens. Forty-two complaints alleging police misconduct in contacts with citizens were sustained.* Despite these facts, the impression that citizen complaints are ignored continues because of deficiencies in the existing procedure. Thus, the clamor is raised from many sources for an independent civilian review board.

The Commission feels that a civilian review board, authorized to investigate, and perhaps to decide, complaints, but with no other law enforcement responsibilities, would endanger the effectiveness of law enforcement, which would be intolerable at a time when crime is on the increase throughout the country. Experience in two cities which have such boards — and in which alleged misconduct of police officers

---

* Of the 42 complaints which were sustained, 10 were for alleged excessive force, 23 were for alleged discourtesy or profanity, and nine alleged unlawful arrest or unreasonable search. In 1964, 470 officers, approximately 10% of the police force, were assessed disciplinary penalties of some type.

was a major issue in connection with riots which occurred in those cities in 1964 — has not demonstrated the advantages of such a review board. From our observations and from testimony of knowledgeable law enforcement administrators, we are persuaded that the value of an independent board would not outweigh the likely deleterious effects on law enforcement. We, therefore, propose improvements in the existing procedure which will go far toward establishing the widest possible confidence in the handling of all complaints but which will not destroy the authority vested by the City Charter in the Board of Police Commissioners and the Chief of Police.

To insure independent investigation of complaints, we recommend that an "Inspector General" should be established in the Police Department, under the authority of the Chief of Police but outside the chain of command. Properly staffed with sworn officers and civilian personnel, the Inspector General would perform the functions of the present Internal Affairs Division and would be responsible for making investigations and recommendations on all citizen complaints, whether filed with the Board or the Department. An adequate hearing process for the complainant should be made available at some point in the procedure, and he should be informed of the action taken on his complaint. The "Inspector General" concept has proved, through years of experience, to be effective in the four military services, each of which has such an independent and objective agency under the Chief of Staff of the service. The Inspector General's investigations can be visible to the public. He would report to the Chief of Police, and his findings and recommendations on all complaints would be the basis for the Chief's report to the Board on all such complaints. The Board would act on all complaints as it now acts on some complaints initially presented to it; that is, it would pass on whether the complaint is or is not sustained. Under the procedure suggested here, responsibility for discipline would remain with the Chief of Police and the Board of Rights as provided by the City Charter.

These improvements, we believe, would provide a satisfactory procedure for processing citizen complaints both from the viewpoint of the Los Angeles Police Department and the community. We have focused our discussion on the existing procedure in the Police Department. We encourage the Los Angeles Sheriff's Department to adopt those aspects of our conclusions which may be applicable to its procedures for handling citizen complaints.

Community-Police Relations —
A Responsibility for Crime Prevention

In 1963, the Los Angeles Police Department issued an excellent statement of the need for and purpose of a community relations program. The order stated:

"The mutual advantages of a friendly relationship between the people of a community and their police force should be widely understood and more fully appreciated. The success of a police force in the performance of its duties is largely measured by the degree of support and cooperation it receives from the people it serves. It is of paramount importance, therefore, to secure for this department the confidence, respect, and approbation of the public. The cultivation of such desirable attitudes on the part of the public is dependent upon reciprocal attitudes on the part of this department."

Witness after witness, in discussing the question of police-community relations, emphasized the importance of "non-punitive contacts" as basic to the problem. But, from the statements of many witnesses it appears that the steps taken by the Los Angeles Police Department, although commendable, have been faltering. The worthwhile Deputy Auxiliary Police program, which was designed to bring youth into closer contact with police organizations, has been permitted to lapse and pass out of existence. The staff assigned to community relations activities is not large enough, and the range of community relations activities has been limited.

Moreover, little has been done in recent years to encourage the Negro youth's support of the police, or to implant in the youth's mind the true value of the Police Department with respect to the welfare of the youth. Productive programs can and must be developed in Los Angeles, as they have been developed elsewhere.

We commend the Board of Police Commissioners and the Chief of Police for the community relations activities which the Department has undertaken in 1965. These have included the appointment of a Coordinator of Community Relations Activity and a Community-Police Relations Advisory Committee, and an increase in the staff of the community relations unit. Visitation programs to elementary schools and command level seminars on community relations have also been useful steps. But, we believe, a greater effort is indicated.

We propose more intensive in-service human relations training programs for officer personnel; youth programs such as the Deputy Auxiliary Police program; periodic open forums and workshops in which the police and residents of the minority communities will engage in discussions of law enforcement; and frequent contact between the police and the students in junior and senior high schools.

Such programs are a basic responsibility of the Police Department. They serve to prevent crime, and, in the opinion of this Commission, crime prevention is a responsibility of the Police Department, equal in importance to law enforcement.

Programs of this nature, and the underlying philosophies that support them, can only be initiated through determined leadership at the top. If these actions are pursued energetically, we can expect a gratifying improvement in the relationship between the police and the community. Successful implementation of these programs will require additional personnel and funds and we believe that the City Council should authorize both without delay.

Again, while we have focused our discussion on the Police Department, we encourage the Los Angeles Sheriff's Department to introduce community relations activities of the character we have recommended for the Police Department.

More Negroes and Mexican-Americans Must Enter Careers in Law Enforcement

Finally, the Commission expresses its concern over the relatively few sworn officer personnel in the Police Department and the Sheriff's Department who are Negroes or Mexican-Americans. Only four percent of the sworn personnel of the Police Department and six percent of the Sheriff's Department are Negroes and an even smaller percentage are Mexican-American. Both of these departments recruit their personnel through the civil service agencies and selections are made on a basis of qualifications without regard for race, religion, or national origin. Despite efforts by the civil service agencies, the law enforcement departments, and some elected officials to encourage Negroes and Mexican-Americans to enter the law enforcement field, the results have been unsatisfactory.

We believe it essential that the number of sworn officers of each minority group should be increased substantially. To bring this about, more active recruitment by the Police and Sheriff's Departments and the civil service must be undertaken. Furthermore, educational and private institutions and organizations, and political leaders as well, should encourage members of the minority groups to enter careers in law enforcement. Finally, budget support for extensive efforts in recruitment, which should perhaps include pre-employment preparatory training, should be provided by both the City Council and the Board of Supervisors.

To implement our conclusions, we offer the following recommendations:

1) The Board of Police Commissioners should be strengthened.

2) Investigations of all citizen complaints should be conducted by an independent Inspector General under the authority of the Chief of Police in the implementation of procedures established by the Board of Police Commissioners.

3) The Police Department should institute expanded community relations programs.

4) The Sheriff's Department should effectuate these recommendations to the extent that they are applicable to it.

EMPLOYMENT — KEY TO INDEPENDENCE

Unemployment — The Immediate Problem

The most serious immediate problem that faces the Negro in our community is employment — securing and holding a job that provides him an opportunity for livelihood, a chance to earn the means to support himself and his family, a dignity, and a reason to feel that he is a member of our community in a true and a very real sense. Unemployment and the consequent idleness are at the root of many of the problems we discuss in this report. Many witnesses have described to us, dramatically and we believe honestly, the overwhelming hopelessness that comes when a man's efforts to find a job come to naught. Inevitably, there is despair and a deep resentment of a society which he feels has turned its back upon him. Welfare does not change this. It provides the necessities of life, but adds nothing to a man's stature, nor relieves the frustrations that grow. In short, the price for public assistance is loss of human dignity.

The welfare program that provides for his children is administered so that it injures his position as the head of his household, because aid is supplied with less restraint to a family headed by a woman, married or unmarried. Thus, the unemployed male often finds it to his family's advantage to drift away and leave the family to fend for itself. Once he goes, the family unit is broken and is seldom restored. Changes in welfare administration designed to hold together rather than break apart the family have not been wholly successful.

From unemployment, other problems develop. In a discouraged frame of mind, the unemployed is driven toward anti-social behavior. Even if he remains at home, he neither serves as a worthy example to his children nor does he actively motivate them to go to school and study. Thus, a chain reaction takes place. The despair and disillusionment of the unemployed parent is passed down to the children. The example of failure is vividly present and the parent's frustrations and habits become the children's. ("Go to school for what?" one youngster said to us.)

There is no immediate total solution to this problem, but it is our opinion that far more can be done than is now being done by government, by the private business sector, by organized labor, and by the Negro community, individually and jointly, to find jobs in the short range and in the long range to train Negroes so that a high proportion of them will not remain out of work.

Government job efforts. Government authorities have recognized the problem and have moved to solve it. City, county, state and federal governments have helped to siphon off some of the distress by hiring high proportions of Negroes. For example, 25% of all new Los Angeles county employees in 1964 were Negro.

Other government programs have been initiated and more have been proposed. These are designed to provide immediate full time and part time employment of the qualified plus training for the unqualified. As examples, under the War on Poverty Program, the Job Corps has provided a full-time work-training program for 363 youths. The Neighborhood Youth Corps has provided part time work for over 1500 youths from the south central area. Also, the Neighborhood Adult Participation Project has constructively employed over 400 in Los Angeles and this number is scheduled to double in the near future.

More recently, and perhaps belatedly, the State Department of Employment, using funds provided by the U. S. Department of Labor, has opened Youth Opportunity Centers to counsel youths in disadvantaged areas and assist them in finding employment. Also, the State Employment Service has recently opened an office in Watts to provide more convenient job placement service to nearby residents.

A disproportionate number of Negroes are presently being rejected for military service because of their inability to meet the relatively high standards insisted upon by the armed services. This raises the question of a reappraisal of recruitment and selective service standards to determine whether they are unnecessarily restrictive. Can they be revised to enable the military service to make a larger contribution to relieving the plight of the Negro without jeopardizing its standards of efficiency?

The Government employment programs are commendable and each in its way has helped to alleviate the problem but they are far from adequate. The critical problem persists.

Advanced billing with respect to federal programs has created a false impression that more job opportunities would be available than actually have developed. The endless bickering between city, state and federal government officials over the administration of the authorized programs — most particularly the Poverty Program — has disappointed many. Yet serious as has been this controversy, we doubt the delay caused by the argument has been of major consequence, except for its psychological effects. The wheels of bureaucracy grind slowly, the claimants on the limited available dollar are countless, and since no priority system exists, long periods of time are necessarily consumed in evaluating programs at the local, state and Washington level before funds are provided. One advocate of a training program told us that when he presented his program to the local anti-poverty office, he found that his project was number 158 in line and consideration could not be expected for about seven months. All of this is understandable; projects are numerous and hope for support is great, but nevertheless, reasonable supervision of the federal purse requires time.

The magnitude of the unemployment problem among Negroes in Los Angeles is difficult to assess, but a reasonable approximation is possible. The total number of unemployed in the county is about 160,000. It is clear that unemployment in the Negro community is two to three times that in the white community; from all indications, there are some 25,000 unemployed Negroes in the central section of Los Angeles County and probably an equal number of unemployed Mexican-Americans.

After studying current governmental employment programs, as well as a number of those proposed for the future, we conclude that the serious unemployment problem of the disadvantaged groups will not soon, or perhaps ever, be alleviated by all of them put together. Other more imaginative and more dynamic plans must be developed and must go forward. This means all private employers must make a more constructive effort to give the qualified Negro an equal opportunity for a job he is able to fill, and they and organized labor must make a massive effort to raise the qualifications of the unqualified through sizable training programs.

A California proposal. Failure of these programs to provide enough jobs led Governor Brown to order a survey of the state to determine how many useful jobs could be created. His survey found many in such fields as law enforcement, education, public health, and conservation. Thus, he advocated a national program estimated to cost the federal government 2.5 billion dollars annually ($250,000,000 for California) which would provide some 50,000 jobs within our state and a proportionate number of jobs elsewhere throughout the nation. An equal amount of money would be needed each year the program continues. Obviously such a program is bound to encounter tough sledding in Washington, especially as the Vietnam costs escalate, and one can readily imagine that months, if not a year or two, might pass before approval would be given and money made available, if it ever is. Since we are somewhat skeptical about the feasibility of this program (especially as to the capacity of the unemployed in the disadvantaged areas to fulfill the jobs specified), we feel that it should be tested on a pilot basis before any massive program is launched. In any event, because there will inevitably be a delay in commencing such a program, we are persuaded that other steps must be taken now.

Training programs. Existing training programs are many. They are authorized and funded by both the federal and state governments and are administered by several separate agencies — the Department of Labor, the Department of Health, Education and Welfare, and the Office of Economic Opportunity. The main source of financing for vocational training is the Manpower Development and Training Act of 1962 (MDTA), which has provided funds for vocational training, both institutional and on the job. Programs under this act have established high entrance requirements and are primarily conducted in the classroom. Thus, training under the act skims the cream of the unemployed, and unfortunately it seldom includes the most disadvantaged. Programs funded wholly or in part by MDTA include: The Youth Training and Employment Projects, supervised by the Economic and Youth Opportunities Agency (a product of the War on Poverty); institutional vocational training administered by the State Department of Employment; On-the-Job Training administered by the Division of Apprenticeship Standards; and numerous other public and private programs to which grants have been made. A distinct type of training is the apprenticeship training which is offered throughout the State of California under the jurisdiction of the Division of Apprenticeship Standards. In addition, state and federal legislation has empowered the Department of Social Welfare and the Bureau of Public Assistance to conduct vocational training for potential employables on the relief rolls.

All of these programs are worthwhile and, if properly administered, contribute constructively to a partial solution to the unemployment problem. But the very diversity of approaches reflected in this listing of programs points up the importance of coordination. Although many different types of unemployed are being reached, the several programs are not visible, and all of the needy are not as well informed as they should be concerning their purpose and existence. This fault, we believe, could be remedied by establishment of permanent and convenient local centers where many of the programs will be located and the unemployed can go for desired and necessary training. We find that, largely because of dispersal, the programs now in existence are not being used to do the most good for the most distressed.

In most programs, two essential elements seem to be missing. The first is "attitudinal training" to help the candidate develop the necessary motivation, certain basic principles of conduct, and essential communication skills, all of which are necessary for success in the training course and for the employment to follow. The second is counseling, a service necessary if use is to be made of the particular skills, interest and attitudes of the candidate. These deficiencies appear to occur principally for budgetary reasons.

Finally, there is an apparent lack of coordination between many of the training programs and the job opportunities. All too often a youth in the south central area goes through training, acquires the necessary skill to fill a job only to find that no job awaits him. The results are disastrous. ("Train for what?" he says to his friends.)

A contributing factor to this situation is the attitude of some labor unions. Some of them contend training programs should not be initiated or conducted in areas where apprenticeship programs exist or where, in their view, there is an adequate supply of union members. This we believe is an unnecessary and self-serving restriction which, in time, will harm the national interest. The unavailability of skilled and semi-skilled workers, already in short supply, might readily retard the expansion of our economy. The President's Manpower Report both for 1964 and 1965 demonstrates an urgent need for skilled and semi-skilled workers for the rest of this decade. This need should generate additional training programs in occupational areas where restrictions now bar the way.

Private efforts. We commend the work of the Los Angeles Chamber of Commerce through its Rehabilitation Committee, under the chairmanship of Mr. H. C. McClellan. This committee organized 100 employers and, through their efforts, over 1,200 Negroes have been employed by private industry in recent months. It is the hope of our Commission that all of the 1,000 or more major employers in the metropolitan area will join this cooperative effort. We urge that a permanent organization, properly staffed and financed by the Chamber of Commerce, be established for this purpose. The committee, as well as several major employers, should continue to operate, in conjunction with the State Employment Service in the south central area and the committee of Negro businessmen, and should establish joint counseling and employment functions, so that those who seek jobs can make application with a minimum of inconvenience and expense.

A proposal for additional action. The great majority of the unemployed in the south central Los Angeles area are unemployable because they lack skill and training. To meet that pressing need, a major job training and placement program should be initiated in the area. This program should be large and should be concentrated in an area which is predominantly Negro.

To be successful, this program must be organized by the Negroes themselves. It must be their program. An organization created by Negro leadership can best encourage the unemployed, most particularly the young men and women who may lack both education and motivation, to come forward and train for the opportunities that will be opened up to them. The initiation of the program by the Negroes themselves should insure that it is well received.

Private employers and unions should support such a move by supplying the necessary equipment, counseling service and in some instances, instructors. Courses should be directed toward job availability and the employers should take upon their shoulders the responsibility of providing jobs to the graduates. Funds will be needed for physical facilities and for operations, and these can be provided under existing legislation such as the Economic Opportunity Act and Manpower Development and Training Act. A good example of such a program is the Opportunities Industrialization Center (OIC), which has been in successful operation in Philadelphia for some time.

Compensation should not be necessary for those trainees who are receiving welfare support. If, on the other hand, the trainee receives no welfare and has no means for his livelihood, then a minimum compensation would be essential during the training program.

Through such a program, we believe that this community, which employs three million men and women, can make a real dent in the unemployment problem. Furthermore, we feel that industry, which faces a problem of scarcity of skilled and semi-skilled workers in certain areas, would be inestimably benefited by such a program. We do not dismiss the importance of the current programs which we have discussed — those providing immediate employment or those providing training for future employment. What is suggested here is vitally necessary and will both complement and enlarge upon existing programs.

The short range program for hiring the qualified unemployed, and the longer range program for training others for later employment, is dependent for its success on the motivation of the Negro and the ability of the Negro to compete with all other applicants for the available jobs. The cooperation we urge between industry, labor unions and members of the Negro community, necessary for the accomplishment of these programs, will be futile unless the individual, when trained, can stand up in our competitive society.

An End to Discrimination

It is the Commission's opinion that both willful and unwitting discrimination in employment have existed and continue to exist within our community. There is an opinion among many employers that the lack of skill and motivation on the part of many Negroes makes them undependable employees, and thus preference is given to those of other ethnic backgrounds. In addition, in many labor unions, past practices, which are extremely difficult to modify or reverse, result in discrimination against the Negroes, especially in the building trade unions and in many apprenticeship programs. Fortunately, in many instances the attitudes on the part of both the employer and labor union leaders have changed in recent years and months, and this has appreciably reduced discrimination against the minorities. Nevertheless, a greater and more conscientious effort on the part of business and labor is essential if the problem of discrimination is to be solved.

To that end, we advocate legislation to empower the California Fair Employment Practices Commission (FEPC) to initiate a program under which all employers of more than 250 workers will be required to file reports, at least annually, listing their total employment and the percentage of Negroes, Mexican-Americans, and other identifiable minority groups by occupational category. Likewise, all labor unions should file reports giving comparable information with respect to their total membership within the state. Such a procedure will afford an accurate insight into the progress which is being made by employers and labor unions in the elimination of discrimination.

THE BURNING. These fires (above) set on Friday, are typical businesses which were destroyed. As the store in Watts (top) burns, looters enter while firemen fight the blaze. The Safeway store (bottom) was one of 70 markets fired.

Color photos by Co Rentmeester Copyright Time Inc.

OVER-ALL LOOK. This aerial view of the scene shows ravaged buildings (bottom) and two buildings on Avalon Boulevard (top), the one at left at 107th Street already burned and gutted, and the one at 108th erupting in smoke and flame.

FRIDAY THE 13TH. The riots were so out of hand on Friday afternoon that looters (bottom) were able to get away with shopping carts full of goods in front of firemen. The first Guardsmen in the area made a sweep (top) that evening.
Color photos by Co Rentmeester Copyright Time Inc.

THE SWEEPS. On Saturday morning (top) Guardsmen and Los Angeles Police marched down Avalon Boulevard to clear the street. Firemen were finally able to begin quelling blazes when Guardsmen rode "shotgun" (bottom) and protected them.

THE LOOTING. During the riots about 40 liquor stores were looted and burned. On Friday afternoon, the youth in blue shirt and dark blue shorts enters a store empty-handed (top) and emerges with a rifle (bottom).

Color photos by Co Rentmeester Copyright Time Inc.

THE EVIDENCE. The extensive sniping and looted weapons were a major problem as this collection of seized guns (top) vividly illustrates. The overturned cars (bottom) show the fury of the riot at its peak.

Photos Copyright The Los Angeles Times

THE MOP-UP. Massive activity by National Guardsmen brought the riot under control. Here they patrol in small groups along the now quiet streets in the early morning to prevent further outbreaks.

Color photos by Co Rentmeester Copyright Time Inc.

Photo Copyright The Los Angeles Times

No law forbids the employer or labor union from maintaining records of the ethnic background of their work force or membership. Some employers have complained that they do not keep such records because they fear the information will, in some way, be used against them. The FEPC must make a special effort to dispel the fear held by some employers that it would attempt to force the employment of specified percentages of minority workers irrespective of qualifications. Since the employer lives in a competitive environment, the FEPC and its administrators must hold to the principle of equality in opportunity based upon the ability of the individual rather than merely on numbers of minority workers employed.

In making this recommendation, we believe that if the maximum degree of cooperation from employers and labor unions is to be achieved, FEPC and other agencies dealing with discriminatory employment practices must continue to rely heavily on persuasion and education in the affirmative action programs. These are the techniques that have been most successful in the past.

Arrest records. Evidence gathered by the Commission's staff indicates that a job applicant with an arrest record faces an additional burden in finding employment. While security considerations sometimes preclude hiring an applicant with an arrest record, blanket rejection of such persons without regard for the nature of the arrest or whether there has been a conviction should be discouraged. We urge employers to re-assess job qualifications with a view to considering whether it is feasible to increase employment opportunities for persons with arrest records.

In light of the foregoing considerations, we recommend:

1. **There should immediately be developed in the affected area a job training and placement center through the combined efforts of Negroes, employers, labor unions, and government.**

2. Federal and state governments should seek to insure, through the development of new facilities and additional means of communication, that maximum advantage is taken of government and private training programs and employment opportunities in our disadvantaged communities.

3. Legislation should be enacted requiring employers with more than 250 employees and all labor unions to report annually to the State Fair Employment Practices Commission the racial composition of their work force and membership.

EDUCATION — OUR FUNDAMENTAL RESOURCE

Education is the keystone of democracy. It provides communication between the diverse elements of our complex society and aids in the elimination of barriers of race and religion. It holds the greatest promise for breaking the cycle of failure which is at the core of the problems of the disadvantaged area. Hope centers on education.

Having recognized this early in our investigation, we launched an in-depth study to determine the quality of education offered in the public schools in the riot area and in other areas of the city. A comparison was made between schools in the riot area (and other disadvantaged areas of the city) and schools in other sections of the city (citywide, and in an advantaged area). Five study areas were selected within the Los Angeles City Unified School District. Four of these are disadvantaged areas: Watts and Avalon (predominantly Negro and within the riot area), and Boyle Heights and East Los Angeles (predominantly Mexican-American and outside the riot area). The other study area included Pacific Palisades, Westwood, and Brentwood, which are, by comparison, advantaged areas.* Citywide data were also compiled.

---

* Watts, Avalon, Boyle Heights, and East Los Angeles are four of 136 geographical study areas in Los Angeles County designated by the Welfare Planning Council, Los Angeles Region, and rank least favorably in the county with respect to the following criteria: family income, male unemployment, education, family status, housing, the ratio of youth and aged to productive adults, and the status of youth in terms of neglect and delinquency. Pacific Palisades, Westwood, and Brentwood are areas in Los Angeles that have the most favorable rankings, relative to the remainder of the county, with respect to the above-mentioned criteria. These data, based on the 1960 census and other sources, are contained in the Welfare Planning Council's publication *Social Profiles: Los Angeles County*, Research Report No. 21 (July 1, 1965).

Achievement in the Disadvantaged Areas

Are the students in the disadvantaged areas able to read and write? Achievement test scores of students in the study areas provide a distressing answer. Average achievement test scores for students in disadvantaged areas were shockingly lower than citywide and advantaged area averages in *all* subjects and at *all* grade levels. Table 1 shows that the average student in disadvantaged areas ranks in the lowest 18th to 24th percentile of the national fifth-grade test population in reading vocabulary and reading comprehension; that is, roughly 80% of the national fifth-grade population achieves better in reading than he does.

Table 1

AVERAGE READING PERFORMANCE IN
COMPARISON AREAS - GRADE B5

Area	Reading Vocabulary Ranking	Reading Comprehension Ranking
Citywide	48	48
Advantaged Area	81	75
Disadvantaged Area — Watts	20	24
Disadvantaged Area — Avalon	20	21
Disadvantaged Area — Boyle Heights	18	19
Disadvantaged Area — East Los Angeles	18	24

On the basis of these scores, it appears that the average student in the fifth grade in schools in the disadvantaged areas is unable to read and understand his textbook materials, to read and understand a daily newspaper, or to make use of reading and writing for ordinary purposes in his daily life. This degree of illiteracy seriously impairs his ability to profit from further schooling.

We examined the scores made on achievement tests given to students in the eighth grade. Their melancholy message, as shown in

Table 2, is that the relative achievement of eighth grade students in the disadvantaged areas is even lower than in the fifth grade.

Table 2

AVERAGE READING PERFORMANCE IN
COMPARISON AREAS - GRADE B8

Area	Reading Vocabulary Ranking	Reading Comprehension Ranking
Citywide	49	47
Advantaged Area	79	77
Disadvantaged Area — Watts	13	16
Disadvantaged Area — Avalon	14	15
Disadvantaged Area — Boyle Heights	15	20
Disadvantaged Area — East Los Angeles	16	17

Table 2 shows that early reading retardation apparently results in students falling further behind as they continue in school.

Table 3 indicates that in the eleventh grade, average reading achievement continues to be significantly below the citywide average.

Table 3

AVERAGE READING PERFORMANCE IN
COMPARISON AREAS - GRADE B11

Area	Reading Vocabulary Ranking	Reading Comprehension Ranking
Citywide	63	55
Advantaged Area	82	73
Disadvantaged Area — Watts	27	24
Disadvantaged Area — Avalon	32	29
Disadvantaged Area — Boyle Heights	34	29
Disadvantaged Area — East Los Angeles	33	30

This is so even though many of the low achievers in the disad
vantaged areas have already dropped out of school by the eleventh
grade, and their absence from the statistics tends to bring up the
average scores. Currently, in the Los Angeles City School District
about 30% of children entering the ninth grade drop out before com
pleting high school. Dropout rates (percentage of average yearly at
tendance) show that three of the high schools that serve students who
reside in disadvantaged areas of south central Los Angeles have the
highest percentage of dropouts of the 45 senior high schools. In these
three schools in predominantly Negro areas, about two-thirds of the
students who enter drop out before graduating from high school.

Since the average achievement of students in the disadvantaged
areas is lower than citywide achievement, it was not surprising that
we found that their intelligence test scores were also lower. To a great
extent, school intelligence tests measure the same abilities as achieve
ment tests. Contrary to what many people believe, intelligence test
do not measure only inborn mental ability; they measure *present* ability
at the time of the test, which is heavily affected by acquired verbal
ability and by cultural-environmental experiences. Students with high
inherent potential may do poorly on intelligence tests if they lack the
background that the tests require.*

Essentially, the reading and writing level of students in the dis
advantaged areas is far too low for them either to advance in school
or to function effectively in society. The frequent direct consequence
of illiteracy are delinquency, welfare problems, unemployment, poverty
and political and social isolation. What are the causes of this in
ability to read? Are the schools discriminating against children in

---

* To whatever extent these intelligence tests do measure potential for learning
the average scores of students in the disadvantaged areas are not so low as to
indicate that these students cannot learn to read and write, if given the proper
educational experience.

disadvantaged areas? How do educational services in disadvantaged areas compare with the services in schools in other areas? Are there environmental factors outside the schools that are related to low achievement? These are the fundamental questions, and the Commission investigated each.

Educational Services in Disadvantaged Areas

The Commission's study compared the quality of educational services offered by the schools in the advantaged and disadvantaged areas. Comparisons were made of class size, teacher qualifications, physical facilities, counseling and special services, curricula, and instructional materials. The Commission then considered whether the quality of these school services could account for differences in achievement of students in schools in advantaged and disadvantaged areas.

Class size. Comparisons of pupil-teacher ratios in advantaged and disadvantaged areas indicate that the average class size tends to be about the same or slightly smaller for schools in disadvantaged areas.

Teacher qualifications. Teachers in the advantaged areas have an average of almost three years more teaching experience in the Los Angeles City Schools than teachers in the disadvantaged areas (7 as compared with almost 10 years). This is reflected by the lower proportion of teachers with permanent status (tenure) in schools in the disadvantaged areas. Two factors appear to account for these differences: first, more experienced teachers tend to move to schools in more advantaged areas; and second, disadvantaged areas tend to be high enrollment growth areas with more new non-permanent teachers assigned to the added classrooms. However, in both the advantaged and disadvantaged areas, teachers have about the same years (4-5 years) of experience in the school where they are now teaching.

Double sessions. Overcrowding is a significant problem in some elementary schools in the Los Angeles City Schools. In these schools the same classroom must be used for two consecutive shifts of students. Although double sessions exist in all subdivisions of the entire school system, the disadvantaged areas have more double sessions than any other part of the city. During the current school year more than three-quarters of the 26,200 students on double sessions attend schools where the enrollment is predominantly Negro or Mexican-American. For example, of the 58 schools in the West District (one of the subdivisions of the Los Angeles Unified School District), 12 have double-session classes; the enrollment in all 12 of these schools is predominantly Negro. The problem of overcrowding has been caused primarily by two factors: high enrollment growth and renovation of classrooms in older buildings in the disadvantaged areas. In our view, the incidence of double sessions is not the product of invidious discrimination.

Currently, in the Los Angeles City Schools, there are 328 unused classrooms in regular elementary schools. We urge the School Board to consider whether there are not practical ways to lessen double sessions by arranging for children whose school is overcrowded to attend nearby schools with unused classrooms.

School buildings. Are the school buildings better in the advantaged areas? The ratio of permanent to temporary buildings shows a slight advantage for the schools in disadvantaged areas. However, the inescapable fact is that many school buildings in disadvantaged areas are older, since they are in older sections of the city. Many of these older buildings require renovation to meet safety standards. On the other hand, new schools have been built, new facilities have been added to older schools, and school buildings have been modernized in the curfew area, as funds were available. Moreover, main-

-62-

enance, refurbishing, repainting, equipping, and custodial care sched-
ules appear to be uniform throughout the district.

Cafeterias. Of the 429 Los Angeles regular elementary schools,
114 are not currently operating cafeterias. Almost two-thirds (71) of
these schools are located in the East, North, and South Districts, which
include most of the schools in the city with predominantly Negro or
Mexican-American enrollment. A major reason for the lack of school
cafeterias is the policy adopted by the Los Angeles City Schools which
requires school cafeterias to be self-supporting and to serve a minimum
number of meals. In addition, no bond funds have been allocated for
construction of cafeterias since 1958. Even in those schools where there
are cafeterias, the Los Angeles City Schools do not provide free or
reduced-price lunches to needy students. An adequate mid-day meal
is essential to a meaningful educational experience. Action should be
taken to provide cafeteria facilities and free or reduced-price meals for
needy students in disadvantaged areas.

Libraries. Some schools in the disadvantaged study areas do not
have libraries while all schools in the advantaged study areas have
libraries. In part, lack of libraries is due to the utilization of rooms to
meet rapid enrollment growth and to house special classes. Libraries
should be provided in all schools.

Counseling and special services. At both the elementary and
secondary levels there are fewer students per counselor in the disadvantaged areas than in the advantaged areas, and there are also more
special services (such as remedial reading, compensatory education,
and social adjustment) offered in the disadvantaged areas. Nevertheless, the counseling and special services for students in the disadvantaged
area are inadequate to meet the need and should be augmented.

Curricula. Because of the higher achievement level of their students, schools in advantaged areas offer a wider variety of advanced

—63—

courses. There are more honors courses, advanced placement courses, and programs at nearby colleges and universities for the academically talented and gifted students in advantaged areas than in disadvantaged areas. The Commission believes that adequate special provisions should be made for all academically talented and gifted students to attend advanced courses. Where necessary, transportation should be provided so that these students may participate in advanced programs offered in other high schools or in universities.

Instructional materials. Instructional materials, including text books and audio-visual aids, are provided on an approximately equal basis. Where there are differences, they favor the disadvantaged areas. The total expenditure for instructional materials is higher per student in the disadvantaged areas than it is in the advantaged areas.

In summary, it appears that inequalities exist with respect to incidence of double sessions, cafeterias, libraries, and course offerings for academically talented students. These differences can and should be eliminated. However, the Commission does not feel that these inequalities or the differences in teacher experience or status fully explain the lower achievement of students in disadvantaged areas.

Environmental Factors

There is increasing evidence to indicate that children who live in disadvantaged areas begin school with a deficiency in environmental experiences which are essential for learning. Several factors outside the school itself appear to relate to low achievement in school, such as the level of education of adults in disadvantaged area communities, mobility, and disciplinary and law enforcement problems.

The educational level of any community and of parents substantially influences the achievement of children in school. There is a serious educational deficit in the adult population in disadvantaged eas. According to the 1960 census, about two-thirds of the adults the disadvantaged areas had failed to graduate from high school. addition, a high percentage (almost 14%) of the adults living in e four study areas were classified as functional illiterates (defined completing less than five years of school). Adding to the problem education has been the tremendous inmigration of Negroes from e South where educational opportunities are limited.

Rapidly increasing school enrollment and high population mobility so characterize the disadvantaged areas. The lack of stability in ese communities is reflected in extremely high student transiency, that n impair both the learning ability of students and the effectiveness teachers. In addition, many schools in the disadvantaged areas are ced with serious disciplinary problems and with disturbing condi- ons in the neighborhood that can also affect the educational achieve- ent of students. These conditions include loiterers and distracting nd unsavory elements near school sites. The personal security of oth teachers and students is often threatened. We believe that dequate school personnel should be provided to deal with disciplinary roblems in schools and adequate law enforcement personnel should e provided at or near schools where necessary.

Children in disadvantaged areas are often deprived in their pre- hool years of the necessary foundations for learning. They have ot had the full range of experiences so necessary to the development language in the pre-school years, and hence they are poorly pre- ared to learn when they enter school. Their behavior, their vocabu- ry, their verbal abilities, their experience with ideas, their view adults, of society, of books, of learning, of schools, and of teachers re such as to have a negative impact on their school experience. hus, the disadvantaged child enters school with a serious educational andicap, and because he gets a poor start in school, he drops further ehind as he continues through the grades. His course toward academic failure is already set before he enters school; it is rooted in his earliest childhood experiences. The Commission concludes that this is the basic reason for low achievement in the disadvantaged areas.

The schools in the disadvantaged areas do not provide a program that meets the unique educational needs of culturally disadvantaged children. Although special remedial programs are offered in an attempt to compensate for deficiencies in learning, the *basic* organization and orientation of schools is the same in advantaged and disadvantaged areas. The same educational program for children of unequal background does not provide an equal opportunity for children to learn.

Overcoming Low Achievement

We propose that the programs for the schools in disadvantaged areas be vastly reorganized and strengthened so as to strike at the heart of low achievement and break the cycle of failure. We advocate a new, massive, expensive, and frankly experimental onslaught on the problem of illiteracy. We propose that it be attacked at the time and place where there is an exciting prospect of success.

The program for education which we recommend is designed to raise the scholastic achievement of the average Negro child up to or perhaps above the present average achievement level in the City. We have no hard evidence to prove conclusively that the program advocated in this report will accomplish this purpose. We emphasize that the proposed program is designed to raise the level of educational achievement of many who are far below average and the success of such an effort must be proven and this proof can come only from the results of the program itself. Nevertheless, we believe the objectives so essential to our society that funds, teachers, specialists and supervision should be provided as proposed.

First, school services in disadvantaged areas must be extended own to the ages of three and four, in order to give these children the ackground and reinforcements, particularly in language skills, that ey have not received in their "informal" education prior to school. hese programs for disadvantaged three and four-year-old children ust be provided throughout the regular school year and they must e permanently maintained. Classes must be more than child-care or aby-sitting services; they must be carefully programmed to provide the ackground these children need to develop verbal and language abilities.

Second, class size must be significantly reduced for children now a elementary and junior high schools in disadvantaged areas. In order ɔ maximize opportunity for effective teaching, class size in these chools should be reduced to a maximum of 22; a less drastic reduction rom the present average class of 33 would still be expensive but would ffer much less promise of success. These programs would have to e continued for a minimum of three years in the junior high schools nd six years in the elementary schools.

Third, additional personnel to cope with disturbed and retarded hildren, and special problems of the disadvantaged child should be nade available in these schools. The energies and services of the eacher can be dissipated if she has to work with a myriad of special roblems that are much greater in number and extent than they are n the more advantaged areas. To be effective, the teacher in disad- antaged areas needs much more immediately available help with ;uidance, welfare, health, and social and emotional problems than do eachers in advantaged areas. While all of these services are presently vailable, the need for such services is far greater in these disad- antaged areas.

A sharp reduction in class size, together with provision for special upporting services and materials, would offer teachers a more professionally rewarding assignment and would be likely to attract dedi cated teachers to seek positions in schools in disadvantaged areas. Th Commission's study as well as experience elsewhere support thi conclusion.

If we can provide the most effective possible learning situatior for the student and attract able teachers to teach in these area we will have made the most important step toward solving the prob lem of low educational achievement. It is clear that the propose programs will be costly, but not as costly, however, as failure, de linquency, loss of productive manpower, and social dependency. Ou society cannot afford this great waste of valuable human resources.

It is our belief that raising the level of scholastic achievemen will lessen the trend towards de facto segregation in the schools in th areas into which the Negroes are expanding and, indeed, will tend t reduce all de facto segregation. It is our conclusion that the very lov level of scholastic achievement we observe in the predominately Negro schools contributes to de facto segregation in the schools. In turr school segregation apparently contributes importantly to all de facte segregation. We reason, therefore, that raising the scholastic achieve ment might reverse the entire trend of de facto segregation. Ther is no proof of this and therefore we cannot demonstrate by specifi example that success of the school program we propose will have the effect on de facto segregation within the schools or elsewhere we indi cate as a possibility.

Accordingly, our major recommendations are:

1. **Elementary and junior high schools in the disadvantaged area which have achievement levels substantially below the city aver age should be designated as "Emergency Schools". In each of these schools, an "Emergency Literacy Program" should be established consisting of a drastic reduction in class size to a**

maximum of 22 students and additional supportive personnel to provide special services. It is estimated that this program will cost at least $250 per year per student in addition to present per student costs and exclusive of capital expenditures, and that it must be continued for a minimum of six years for the elementary schools and three years for the junior high schools.

. A permanent pre-school program should be established throughout the school year to provide education beginning at age three. Efforts should be focused on the development of language skills essential to prepare children to learn to read and write.

THE CONSUMER AND THE COMMUTER

The Disadvantaged Consumer

The Commission heard recurrent testimony of alleged consumer exploitation in south central Los Angeles: of higher prices being charged for food there than in other parts of town, of spoiled meat or produce or old bread being sold at the same price as fresh, of high interest rates on furniture and clothing purchases, of shoddy materials at high prices. Complaints were also registered to the effect that there is a bias against the curfew area in the practices of insurance companies and institutional lenders. In a related vein, a number of witnesses advanced the view that there was a vengeance pattern to the destruction of stores in the curfew area, that it was a retribution on merchants who were guilty of consumer exploitation, and particularly on Caucasians who were said to "take from the area but put nothing back into it."

Our study of the patterns of burning and looting does not indicate any significant correlation between alleged consumer exploitation and the destruction. On the contrary, a number of stores with a reputation for ethical practices and efficient and low-priced operation suffered major damage (" . . . the beautiful blocklong market . : . which was 99% Negro staffed, was the second to burn . . ." said one witness), while businesses which were widely unpopular came through the riot unmarked. (Another witness stated, "I hate to say this, but . . . the one they didn't burn — I don't know why they didn't burn that if they were going to burn something — we don't buy anything out of there.") There was some evidence that businesses which were apparently Negro-owned were spared — many by hastily-posted signs such as "Negro-owned", and "Blood brother" — but there is also evidence of the destruction of some Negro-owned businesses.

The consumer problem for many curfew area residents has the double bite of poverty and race. The practices that such residents criticize are a classic pattern in impoverished communities. But the factor of race — the merchants are for the most part white — sometimes leads the curfew area resident to conclude that oppressive or seemingly oppressive practices are directed against him to keep him in his place. Thus, regardless of actual exploitation, the area resident may believe he is exploited. However, our conclusion, based upon an analysis of the testimony before us and on the reports of our consultants, is that the consumer problems in the curfew area are not due to systematic racial discrimination but rather result from the traditional interplay of economic forces in the market place, aggravated by poverty conditions.

We have no doubt, however, that there are serious problems for the consumer in this disadvantaged area, just as there are wherever there is poverty. One is the costly and inadequate transportation from within the south central area to other parts of Los Angeles which tends to restrict residents of that area to the nearby stores, and which we discuss in more detail later in this section. Another problem is "easy credit" which can become harsh indeed if the disadvantaged person defaults on his installment obligations. The debtor may experience the loss of his property through repossession, or the loss of his job through repeated garnishments of his wages. While it is easy to say that the improvident debtor brought this state upon himself, we deplore the tactics of some merchants and lenders who help induce low-income persons to become heavily debt-burdened. Still another problem for the Negro consumer is the lack of an adequate remedy when he feels he has been unfairly treated. Public and private agencies exist to help the consumer in such a situation, but while manned by able and conscientious professionals, these agencies are generally understaffed, underfinanced, and overburdened. Often the consumer does not even know of the agency's existence.

Having considered the consumer problem, we suggest that usef⟨ steps might be taken in the following areas:

1. The Civil Division of the Public Defender's Office might co⟨ sider expanding its services in the curfew area by opening branc⟨ offices and publicizing their availability. The Neighborhood Leg⟨ Services Offices, soon to be opened under the anti-poverty program will provide an additional needed resource. These agencies shoul⟨ consider instituting preventive legal programs to inform the consum⟨ concerning his legal rights.

2. The Better Business Bureau, a private agency which receiv⟨ complaints regarding consumer practices and is active in consum⟨ education, should open a branch office in south central L⟨ Angeles and equip it with a competent staff. More immediatel⟨ courses in consumer education should be expanded in the adult ed⟨ cation schools of the Los Angeles City School System and by the man⟨ volunteer and private groups working in the curfew area. Further, w⟨ encourage law enforcement departments, such as the Consumer Frau⟨ Division of the Attorney General's Office, to investigate vigorously, an⟨ prosecutors to prosecute firmly, those who criminally victimize citizer⟨ in this area.

3. Based upon our informal survey of conditions of sanitation i⟨ food markets in the curfew area, we recommend that the County Healt⟨ Department increase and improve its inspection program for ⁺ᴸ⟨ markets in all disadvantaged areas of the city.

4. We are persuaded that the businessmen in the curfew are⟨ should show a greater interest in the community where they work, or,⟨ already taking an interest, should make more energetic efforts to a⟨ quaint the community with what they are doing. We feel it is imper⟨ tive that positive initiatives be taken immediately by the entire busines⟨ community. In particular, we believe that lending institutions shoul⟨

at Negro borrowers and Negro clients on the basis of each individual's ponsibility rather than establish policies for all members of a race or ographical area irrespective of individual differences.

ansportation

Our investigation has brought into clear focus the fact that the adequate and costly public transportation currently existing through- t the Los Angeles area seriously restricts the residents of the dis- vantaged areas such as south central Los Angeles. This lack of equate transportation handicaps them in seeking and holding jobs, tending schools, shopping, and in fulfilling other needs. It has had a ajor influence in creating a sense of isolation, with its resultant frus- ations, among the residents of south central Los Angeles, particu- rly the Watts area. Moreover, the lack of adequate east-west or rth-south service through Los Angeles hampers not only the resi- nts of the area under consideration here but also of all the city.

Historically, the Los Angeles area was served by private trans- rtation systems, many of which were sold to the Metropolitan Transit uthority, a public entity, in 1958. The Southern California Rapid ransit District (SCRTD), which was created by the legislature, suc- eded the Metropolitan Transit Authority in November 1964. The CRTD, although a public agency, is neither tax supported nor subsi- ized. It operates 1500 buses in a four county area and depends for venue solely upon the fare box. Revenue and expense projections indi- ate the SCRTD will break even or possibly suffer a loss this year and a ss is forecast in future years. Traditionally, bus systems in the Los ngeles area have met increasing costs in operations by increasing fares nd cutting back service. The consequence of these actions has been a ansportation system which is prohibitively expensive and inadequate service.

In general, the coverage and frequency of bus service in the Watts area is comparable to service throughout the Los Angeles area. In the judgment of the Commission, however, it is both inadequate and too costly. As related to the Watts area, the problem stems from the following facts:

(1) Four separate bus entities and one subsidiary operate within the Watts area (Southern California Rapid Transit District, Atkinson Transportation Company and its associated company, South Los Angeles Transportation Company, Torrance Municipal, and Gardena Municipal). These three public entities and one private entity with its subsidiary are by law given exclusive rights to serve within their respective franchised area. A resident of Watts may have to ride on several separate bus systems to reach certain destinations in the immediate area. These transportation systems are uncoordinated, do not provide for free transfers between systems (except in the instance of parent and subsidiary), and have been forced to cut back service and increase fares over the years because of increased capital and operating expenses.

(2) SCRTD is authorized by law to provide long-line services connecting contiguous urban areas, and thus it provides the principal transportation in and out of the Watts area. This system does not have free transfer privileges between most separate urban areas, nor to local services within most contiguous urban areas, many of which maintain their own bus services. This means that transportation from one section of the metropolitan area such as Watts to almost any other area requires an additional fare or fares and transfers.

We believe that adequate and economical public bus transportation is essential to our community and that it should not be ignored because of the debate over mass rapid transit. Indeed, we make a sharp

istinction between mass rapid transit, which is an important issue
icing the people of Los Angeles, and public bus transportation, which
essential without regard to what decision is reached on mass rapid
ansit. Public transportation is particularly essential to the poor and
isadvantaged who are unable to own and operate private automobiles.
Only 14% of the families in Watts are car owners as against at least
0% elsewhere within the Los Angeles County.)

Los Angeles is the only major metropolitan area in the United
tates that does not subsidize the operating losses of its public transpor-
ition in one way or another. By comparison, San Francisco supports
ublic transportation within its city limit by public subsidy which we are
ld amounts to about $10,000,000 per year. If the Los Angeles area
s a whole and the Watts area in particular are to have better bus trans-
ortation service, it can only be provided through a public subsidy to
ccomplish three purposes: reduce fares, purchase or condemn the
ultiple uncoordinated bus system, and provide system-wide transfers.
Ve believe that such a subsidy is justified because of public necessity
nd convenience, and therefore we have no hesitation in recommending

Therefore, recognizing that transportation improvement for the
Vatts area cannot be achieved without similar transportation im-
rovement for the Los Angeles metropolitan area, the Commission
:commends:

(1) A public subsidy in one form or another to give SCRTD
nancial ability to provide an adequate and reasonable bus transpor-
ition system throughout the metropolitan area.

(2) The acquisition by SCRTD of the existing small transpor-
ition companies which now complicate and increase the cost of trans-
ortation in the Los Angeles area.

(3) The establishment of transfer privileges in order to minimize
ransportation costs.

(4) With respect to the Watts area in particular, immediat
establishment of an adequate east-west cross town service as well a
increasing the north-south service to permit efficient transportation t
and from the area.

WELFARE AND HEALTH

ublic Welfare

The public welfare program in Los Angeles County involves an nnual expenditure of over $400 million. Administered by the County ureau of Public Assistance, the program is funded by contributions rom the federal government (42%), the state government (39%), nd the county (19%). The magnitude of this program can be some-vhat better grasped by comparing it with the expenditures under the ederal War on Poverty which will amount to roughly $30 million in he Los Angeles area in 1965. In August 1965, approximately 344,000 ersons or 5% of the county's population received some form of velfare aid. In the same month 94,000 persons or 14% of the total opulation of the curfew area as a whole received public assistance. n the Watts area, approximately 24% of the population received such ssistance.

Six major welfare programs exist in Los Angeles, five financed by he federal, state and county governments (Old Age Security, Aid to he Disabled, Aid to the Blind, Medical Assistance to the Aged, and id to Families with Dependent Children), and one financed by the ounty alone — General Relief. The costliest of these programs are Old Age Security ($125 million per year in 1965) and Aid to Families vith Dependent Children (about $95 million per year in 1965).

The predominant welfare program in the curfew area is the Aid o Families with Dependent Children program (AFDC). Slightly more than two-thirds of all welfare recipients in the curfew area as a vhole, and over 83% of all welfare recipients in the Watts area, eceived assistance under the AFDC program. Broadly speaking, this program provides for payments to a family with a related child under 18 vho has been deprived of support by reason of the absence, incapacity, or unemployment of a father. There are two aspects of the AFDC pro-gram — (1) the AFDC-FG (Family Group) program where the

-77-

family unit is generally headed by a woman and (2) the AFDC-U (Unemployed head) program, authorized by the 1963 legislature t provide for families where there is an unemployed man at the head o the household. Average monthly payments on the AFDC-FG pro gram are $177 per family; on the AFDC-U program, $238 per family

A recent survey indicates that 90% of the AFDC families in th curfew area are Negro. In nine out of 10 of these homes, the father i absent. Over 70% of the parents involved were born in the South o Southwest. Seven out of 10 families on AFDC receive aid for one o more illegitimate children.

In Los Angeles County as a whole, expenditures for the AFDC program have been increasing dramatically, far outrunning the popu lation trends. Between 1960 and 1964, when county population in creased 13%, expenditures for the AFDC program rose by 73%. Be tween 1963 and 1964, when county population increased 2.5% AFDC expenditures increased over 14% from $69.4 million to $79.5 million annually. Expenditures for the new AFDC-U program, which amounted to $10.2 million in 1964, are not included in the foregoing computation and, therefore, do not explain the rapid increases.

We have no intention of opposing the humanitarian purpose of the welfare program. Nevertheless, we are profoundly disturbed by the accelerating trend of expenditure. Our concern is heightened by the fact that this is occurring, not at a time of economic downturn or depression, but during the present period of unparalleled prosperity for our nation and state. A portion of the rapid increase may be ex plained by the fact that the Negro and Mexican-American population in Los Angeles is estimated to have increased approximately 40% in the last five years, compared with the general population increase of 13 percent in the same period. Moreover, the high unemployment in this area, referred to early in this report, no doubt has contributed o the increase. However, the increase in AFDC expenditures, coupled with the increase in population, raises a question in the minds of some whether the generosity of the California welfare program compared with those in the southern and southwestern states is not one of the factors causing the heavy inmigration of disadvantaged people to Los Angeles.*

We are making recommendations in other fields which can assist in lightening the welfare load. The program we are recommending in the field of education will, we believe, have a major impact on unemployment over the long term. We hope our recommendations in the field of employment will have a similar effect in the shorter run. In an important sense, the cost of these programs is justified by their potential for reducing welfare expenses.

However, to be successful in doing so, these programs must be accompanied with a recognition that a truly successful welfare program must, wherever feasible, create an initiative and an incentive on the part of the recipients to become independent of state assistance. Otherwise, the welfare program promotes an attitude of hopelessness and permanent dependence.

After hearing extensive testimony and studying the reports of our consultants, we are convinced that welfare administrators must make a new and vigorous effort to create an initiative and an incentive for independence among welfare recipients. There are some encouraging signs that the philosophy of rehabilitation is being accepted. ("We have about 6,000 people, including the general relief program and the AFDC-U, in some kind of training program," said one administrator.) But we are satisfied that the effort must be doubled and redoubled if any real impact is to be made on the rapidly rising rolls.

---

* A comment regarding this sentence by the Rev. James Edward Jones is set forth at page 87 infra.

We are assured that many of the present recipients would rathe have work than welfare, but the simple arithmetic of the matter make us uncertain. A job at the minimum wage pays about $220 per month against which there would be transportation, clothes and other expense When the average AFDC family receives from $177 to $238 pe month (depending on the program), the financial incentive to fin work may be either negative or non-existent. (Indeed, we were tol that the 18 year old girl who is no longer eligible for assistance whe living with her mother may have considerable incentive to become mother herself so as to be eligible again as the head of a new famil group.)

The evidence before us makes it plain that welfare administrator are frequently at odds with other governmental officials and on another. Serious conflicts and paradoxes in statutes, regulations, an interpretations were called to our attention. We have not been able in the time available, to formulate recommendations regarding thes disputes or to attempt to clarify the rules, but we are concerned tha energy is being diverted to those non-productive areas. We were als told much about the inaccessibility of welfare offices and the poo physical facilities of some. We have been told by some witnesses an by our consultants that these conditions have produced severe irrita tions and frustrations among many individuals in south central Lo Angeles. Studies on these complicated matters have been made i the past and others are being initiated presently by the state goverm ment, which perhaps may help resolve these problems.

For the improvement of the welfare picture, to us the most promis ing prospect is a closer coordination between welfare and relate agencies which may provide avenues to independence. We believe tha there has not been adequate liaison between welfare workers and gov ernment officials involved in employment. (Most welfare recipients are

mployable, we are told by a welfare administrator, but from an employment official we hear the exact opposite.)

Similarly, welfare agencies should be cognizant of the many avail-
ble training programs. From our study of the matter, we believe that
here is much room for improvement here. We also believe that the use
f child care centers to free heads of families for employment or train-
ng should be emphasized. ("Down in that area we have about 2,000
nothers who would like to go into our Community Work and Training
'rograms, but they can't because there is no place to keep their kids,"
n administrator told us.) In sum, we implore welfare administrators
o devote the most serious and pragmatic efforts to create, wherever
easible, additional incentives for welfare recipients to become inde-
endent of public aid.

Health Problems

Statistics indicate that health conditions of the residents of south
central Los Angeles are relatively poor and facilities to provide medical
care are insufficient. Infant mortality, for example, is about one and
one-half times greater than the city-wide average. Life expectancies
are considerably shorter. A far lower percentage of the children are
immunized against diphtheria, whooping cough, tetanus, smallpox, and
poliomyelitis than in the rest of the county.

As established by the comprehensive reports of consultants to the
Commission, the number of doctors in the southeastern part of Los
Angeles is grossly inadequate as compared with other parts of the city.
It is reported that there are 106 physicians for some 252,000 people,
whereas the county ratio is three times higher. The hospitals readily
accessible to the citizens in southeastern Los Angeles are also grossly inadequate in quality and in numbers of beds. Of the eight proprietary
hospitals, which have a total capacity of 454 beds, only two meet
minimum standards of professional quality. The two large public

hospitals, County General and Harbor General, are both distant and difficult to reach. The Commission recognizes that the motivation of patients to take advantage of the available medical facilities is an important factor in health conditions but it appears that the facilities in the area are not even sufficient to care for those who now seek medical attention.

In light of the information presented to it, the Commission believes that immediate and favorable consideration should be given to a new, comprehensively-equipped hospital in this area, which is now under study by various public agencies. To that end we strongly urge that a broadly based committee (including citizens of the area and representatives of the Los Angeles County Department of Charities, Los Angeles County Medical Association, the California Medical Association, the State Department of Health, and medical and public health schools) be appointed to study where such a hospital should be located and to make recommendations upon various technical and administrative matters in connection with the hospital.

We also believe that the Los Angeles County Health Department should increase the number and services of public health and preventive medical facilities in the area and that similar program improvement should be undertaken by the Los Angeles County Department of Mental Health, the Visiting Nurse Association of Los Angeles, and other voluntary health agencies.

NEITHER SLUMS NOR URBAN GEMS

ow it began

World War II marked the commencement of an explosive growth
i Los Angeles' Negro population. In 1940 approximately 75,000
Iegroes lived in the county; by the end of World War II, this figure
ad doubled, as Negroes streamed in to man the assembly lines of Los
ngeles' shipyards and aircraft plants. In the post-war years, the
rowth continued; presently, the county's Negro population stands at
bout 650,000, an almost tenfold increase since 1940.

Of the entire Negro population in Los Angeles, 88.6 percent
esides in areas considered segregated, concentrated for the most part
i the 46.5 square miles of south central Los Angeles placed under
urfew last August. The reasons for the concentration in south central
os Angeles are both legal and historical; they are closely tied to the
rigins of the small portion of the curfew area called Watts.

Once part of an old Mexican land grant named El Rancho
'ajuata, the predecessor of the community of Watts was the small
ettlement of Tajuata. This settlement, which was founded in 1883
vhen the completion of the Santa Fe and Southern Pacific Railroads
aunched a wave of land speculation in Los Angeles, lay on the right-
f-way of the old Los Angeles and San Pedro Railroad.

In the early 1900's, Henry E. Huntington began to construct
he Pacific Electric Railroad, providing transportation throughout the
os Angeles basin. Two of the Pacific Electric's major lines — a north-
outh line running from the center of Los Angeles to Long Beach
nd an east-west line from Santa Ana to Venice — intersected
lose to Tajuata on land which had come into the possession of the Watts
amily. A railroad station was constructed at the intersection and
amed Watts; shortly thereafter, Tajuata's name was changed to Watts.

-83-

With the building of the railroad came the immigration of Mexican laborers, most of whom were employed by Pacific Electric. Since transportation was close at hand and land was cheap, many of the Mexicans settled in Watts, which had been incorporated as an independent city in 1907. About the same time, and probably for the same reasons, a small settlement of Negroes grew up in a portion of Watts called Mudtown.

The population surges and spreads

The First World War brought new immigrants into Los Angeles to fill the jobs opened by new industries. Some of these immigrants were Negroes from southern states, and they too settled in Watts. The Negro population in this area continued to grow during the 1920's and the 1930's, but until World War II the area was about evenly divided among Negros, Mexican-Americans, and other Caucasians. The community remained poor; its incorporation into the City of Los Angeles in 1926 resulted in little change in its economy.

As Los Angeles' Negro population began to spiral upwards in World War II, the new arrivals understandably gravitated to the areas already occupied by Negroes — Central Avenue and Watts. Accentuating the concentration here was the fact that deed restrictions and other forms of discriminatory practices made it extremely difficult, often impossible, for Negroes to purchase or rent homes in many section: of the city and county.

As a result, Watts soon filled up and Negro neighborhoods began to expand in adjacent areas to the north, south and west. As they did, Los Angeles saw Caucasians following the same pattern which other cities had witnessed: They moved out when the Negro population in any particular neighborhood increased to appreciable proportions. Thus over the course of a quarter century did the large majority of the

Negro population in Los Angeles, as elsewhere, come to reside in segregated areas.

In recent years, a small number of local citizen groups west of the Harbor Freeway, notably Crenshaw Neighbors, Inc., have attempted to slow or arrest the exodus of Caucasians from neighborhoods which Negroes are entering. Entirely voluntary, their efforts are founded on increasing mutual communication, understanding, and respect between the races. We commend these groups; they act on the admirable principle that an individual should be judged without reference to race. Nonetheless, they face obvious problems, notably the concern of Caucasian parents that the neighborhood's schools will suffer. We believe that the educational program which we urge elsewhere in this report can, in the long run, materially assist such efforts.

In the early 1950's, construction began on the Harbor Freeway, extending from downtown Los Angeles south to the harbor communities. This freeway intersected the westernmost extremities of the areas into which Negroes were then expanding. Since housing and other conditions were superior west of the freeway, crossing the freeway to live on the west side became an ambition of many Negroes. Most of the Negro leaders who appeared before this Commission reside west of the freeway.

South Central Los Angeles: Living Conditions

What, then, are the living conditions of those who reside in the portion of south central Los Angeles which became part of the curfew area in August of this year? Compared with the conditions under which Negroes live in most other large cities of the United States, Los Angeles conditions are superior. This has been confirmed by witnesses before this Commission who noted, for example, that the majority of dwelling units in Watts are single-family structures and that the streets and lawns are well kept for a poverty area.

This is not to conclude that housing in south central Los Angeles is superb. On the contrary, residents of south central Los Angeles live in conditions inferior to the citywide average and, of course, markedly inferior to the newer sections in West Los Angeles. Structures are older and more of them are sub-standard. Population density is higher; in Watts, for example, there is an average of 4.3 persons per household, compared with an overall county average of 2.94 persons per household.

Much has been done in the past ten or fifteen years to improve the situation. For example, we have been informed that a survey of Watts by the city's Department of Building and Safety resulted in the removal of 2,104 dwelling units which were too dilapidated for occupancy. The Department of Building and Safety states that only three percent of dwelling units now existing in the curfew zone can be classified as dilapidated.

Nor has Los Angeles failed to provide the curfew area with an equal share of public facilities and services. Thirty-nine recreational facilities exist within the area — ten operated by Los Angeles County and the remainder, including nine swimming pools, operated by the city. We are informed that the construction and maintenance of streets in the curfew zone is roughly comparable with that of the total county, as is refuse collection and sanitation. Street lighting meets minimum standards, although it is not as good as in some other areas. City officials inform us that this disparity exists because the lighting may be increased at the request of property owners and merchants in an area, who must agree to be assessed for the extra costs.

A serious deterioration

Nevertheless, we have received extensive testimony expressing residents' dissatisfaction with the area's physical facilities. Of particular concern to us is the fact that a serious deterioration of the area is in progress. Houses are old and require constant maintenance if they are to remain habitable. Over two-thirds of them are owned by absentee landlords. In numerous instances neither landlords nor tenants appear willing to join in a cooperative effort to halt the deterioration. Many landlords are faced with problems of a high turnover in tenants who do not consider themselves responsible for assisting to maintain the property. Tenants resent the high proportion of their income which they must devote to rent for shelter which in many instances is more deteriorated than housing in the total county.

Compounding the problem is the fact that both private financial institutions and the Federal Housing Authority consider the residential multiple unit in the curfew area an unattractive market because of difficult collection problems, high maintenance costs, and a generally depreciating area resulting from the age of surrounding structures. Moreover, unlike cities such as New Haven, Connecticut, private groups have not taken full advantage of the numerous federally supported programs designed to assist the construction of low-cost housing. At the same time, the development of public housing has been limited by the failure of voters to approve governmental development of low-cost housing, as required by the California Constitution.

In view of the deterioration of the area, the Commission urges the implementation of a continuing urban rehabilitation and renewal program for south central Los Angeles. We look with gratification upon the recent action of the City Council in approving an application by the city for federal assistance under the Community Analysis Program to develop and implement a Master Plan.

Nevertheless, all action cannot wait until the completion of the study and, to this end, private non-profit organizations such as churches and unions should be encouraged to sponsor low-cost housing under section 221(d)(3) of the National Housing Act and similar statutes.

The experience of other cities tentatively indicates the possibility that such projects can be integrated if coordinated with a program which rehabilitates the surrounding neighborhood and insures that good schools are available.

We also urge that the regulations of the Federal Housing Authority be revised so as to liberalize credit and area requirements for FHA-insured loans in disadvantaged areas. This would encourage residents to rehabilitate as well as to acquire property in the area. Similarly, we urge that the regulations applicable to savings and loan institutions be revised in order to offer an incentive to such institutions to participate in financing the purchase, development, and rehabilitation of blighted areas.

The Commission also urges that one county-wide "data bank" be created to centralize and standardize the information and statistics which numerous federal, state and local agencies collect concerning various areas of the county. At present no coordinating unit exists, and each agency collects information on geographic, time, and methodological considerations which have little relevance to the considerations employed by other agencies. The result is needless waste, duplication, and confusion, since it is often impossible to correlate one agency's figures with another's.

A SUMMING UP — THE NEED FOR LEADERSHIP

The study of the Los Angeles riots which we have now completed brought us face to face with the deepening problems that confront America. They are the problems of transition created by three decades of change during which the historical pattern of urban and rural life — which for decades before existed side by side, each complementing and supporting the other — has been violently and irreversibly altered. Modern methods and mechanization of the farm have dramatically, and, in some regards, sadly reduced the need for the farm hand. With this, a drift to the city was the inevitable and necessary result. With respect to the Negro, the drift was first to the urban centers of the South and then, because scanty means of livelihood existed there, on northward and westward to the larger metropolitan centers. It was not the Negro alone who drifted; a substantial part of the entire farm labor force, white and Negro alike, was forced to move and did.

World War II and, to a lesser extent, the Korean War of the early '50's, tended to accelerate the movement, particularly the drift of the Negro from the south to the north. Because job opportunities existed in the war plants located in our cities, the deep and provocative problem created by the movement was not at first appreciated by society. Since then, caught up in almost a decade of struggle with civil rights and its related problems, most of America focused its attention upon the problem of the South — and only a few turned their attention and thoughts to the explosive situation of our cities.

But the conditions of life in the urban north and west were sadly disappointing to the rural newcomer, particularly the Negro. Totally untrained, he was qualified only for jobs calling for the lesser skills and these he secured and held onto with great difficulty. Even the jobs he found in the city soon began to disappear as the mechanization of industry took over, as it has since the war, and wiped out one task after another — the only tasks the untrained Negro was equipped to fill.

Hence, equality of opportunity, a privilege he sought and expected, proved more of an illusion than a fact. The Negro found that he entered the competitive life of the city with very real handicaps: he lacked education, training, and experience, and his handicaps were aggravated by racial barriers which were more traditional than legal. He found himself, for reasons for which he had no responsibility and over which he had no control, in a situation in which providing a livelihood for himself and his family was most difficult and at times desperate. Thus, with the passage of time, altogether too often the rural Negro who has come to the city sinks into despair. And many of the younger generation, coming on in great numbers, inherit this feeling but seek release, not in apathy, but in ways which, if allowed to run unchecked, offer nothing but tragedy to America.

Realizing this, our Commission has made, in this report, many costly and extreme recommendations. We make them because we are convinced the Negro can no longer exist, as he has, with the disadvantages which separate him from the rest of society, deprive him of employment, and cause him to drift aimlessly through life.

This, we feel, represents a crisis in our country. In this report, we describe the reasons and recommend remedies, such as establishment of a special school program, creation of training courses, and correction of misunderstandings involving law enforcement. Yet to do all of these things and spend the sums involved will all be for naught unless the conscience of the community, the white and the Negro community together, directs a new and, we believe, revolutionary attitude towards the problems of our city.

This demands a form of leadership that we have not found. The time for bitter recriminations is past. It must be replaced by thoughtful efforts on the part of all to solve the deepening problems that threaten the foundations of our society.

Government. Government authorities have done much and have been generous in their efforts to help the Negro find his place in our society and in our economy. But what has been done is but a beginning and sadly has not always reached those for whom it was intended in time and in a meaningful way. Programs must not be oversold and exaggerated, on the one hand, or unnecessarily delayed on the other. What we urge is a submersion of personal ambition either political or bureaucratic, in the interest of doing the most good and creating the best results from each and every dollar spent in existing programs.

With particular respect to the City of Los Angeles, we urge the immediate creation of a City Human Relations Commission, endowed with clear cut responsibility, properly staffed and adequately funded. We envisage a commission composed of a chairman and six members with special competence in the fields of research, employment, housing, education, law, youth problems and community organizations. This City Commission should develop comprehensive educational programs designed to enlist the cooperation of all groups, both public and private, in eliminating prejudice and discrimination in employment, housing, education, and public accommodations.

Business and Labor. Business leaders have their indispensable role. No longer can the leaders of business discharge their responsibility by merely approving a broadly worded executive order establishing a policy of non-discrimination and equality of opportunity as a basic directive to their managers and personnel departments. They must insist that these policies are carried out and they must keep records to see that they are. Also, they must authorize the necessary facilities for employment and training, properly designed to encourage the employment of Negroes and Mexican-Americans, rather than follow a course which all too often appears to place almost insurmountable hurdles in the path of the Negro or Mexican-American seeking a job. Directly and through the Chamber of Commerce, the Merchants and Manufacturers Association, and other associations, the business leader can play a most important role in helping to solve the crisis in our cities.

Labor unions have their very vital role. Union leaders must be resolute in their determination to eliminate discrimination and provide equality of opportunity for all within spheres of their jurisdiction and influence. For one reason or another, the records of the ethnic mix of the membership of many unions have not been furnished despite our repeated requests. In labor, as in business, pronouncements of policy, however well intended, are not enough. Unless a union conducts its affairs on a basis of absolute equality of opportunity and non-discrimination, we believe there is reason to question its eligibility to represent employees at the bargaining table.

News Media. The press, television, and radio can play their part. Good reporting of constructive efforts in the field of race relations will be a major service to the community. We urge all media to report equally the good and the bad — the accomplishments of Negroes as well as the failures; the assistance offered to Negroes by the public and private sectors as well as the rejections.

In our study of the chronology of the riots, we gave considerable attention to the reporting of inflammatory incidents which occurred in the initial stage of the Los Angeles riots. It is understandably easy to report the dramatic and ignore the constructive; yet the highest traditions of a free press involve responsibility as well as drama. We urge that members of all media meet and consider whether there might be wisdom in the establishment of guide lines, completely voluntary on their part, for reporting of such disasters. Without restricting their essential role of carrying the news to the public fairly and accurately, we believe news media may be able to find a voluntary basis for exercising restraint and prudence in reporting inflammatory incidents. This has been done successfully elsewhere.

The Negro and the leader. Finally, we come to the role of the Negro leader and his responsibility to his own people and to the community in which he lives. The signing of the Voting Rights Act by President Johnson in the spring of 1965 climaxed a long and bitter fight over civil rights. To be sure, the civil rights controversy has never been the issue in our community that it has been in the South. However, the accusations of the leaders of the national movement have been picked up by many local voices and have been echoed throughout the Negro community here. As we have said in the opening chapter of this report, the angry exhortations and the resulting disobedience to law in many parts of our nation appear to have contributed importantly to the feeling of rage which made the Los Angeles riots possible. Although the Commission received much thoughtful and constructive testimony from Negro witnesses, we also heard statements of the most extreme and emotional nature. For the most part, our study fails to support — indeed the evidence disproves — most of the statements made by the extremists. We firmly believe that progress towards ameliorating the current wrongs is difficult in an atmosphere pervaded by these extreme statements.

If the recommendations we make are to succeed, the constructive assistance of all Negro leaders is absolutely essential. No amount of money, no amount of effort, no amount of training will raise the disadvantaged Negro to the position he seeks and should have within this community — a position of equality — unless he himself shoulders a full share of the responsibility for his own well being. The efforts of the Negro leaders, and there are many able and dedicated ones among us, should be directed toward urging and exhorting their followers to this end.*

The Commission recognizes that much of what it has to say about causes and remedies is not new, although it is backed up by fresh additional evidence coming out of the investigation of the Los Angeles riots. At the same time, the Commission believes that there is an urgency in solving the problems, old or new, and that all Americans, whatever their color, must become aware of this urgency. Among the many steps which should be taken to improve the present situation, the Commission affirms again that the three fundamental issues in the urban problems of disadvantaged minorities are: employment, education and police-community relations. Accordingly, the Commission looks upon its recommendations in these three areas as the heart of its plea and the City's best hope.

As we have said earlier in this report, there is no immediate remedy for the problems of the Negro and other disadvantaged in our community. The problems are deep and the remedies are costly and will take time. However, through the implementation of the programs we propose, with the dedication we discuss, and with the leadership we call for from all, our Commission states without dissent, that the tragic violence that occurred during the six days of August will not be repeated.

---

* A comment regarding this by the Rev. James Edward Jones is set forth at p. 87 infra.

COMMENTS OF THE REV. JAMES EDWARD JONES

1. There is the observation at the top of page 71 that the generosity of California welfare programs encourage heavy inmigration of disadvantaged peoples to the Los Angeles area. I have been unable to find statistics to justify this statement and violently disagree with this unjustifiable projection. The report has also stated that Negroes like other disadvantaged peoples have come to Los Angeles to seek the better opportunities offered in an urban area. Welfare programs discourage inmigration to receive public assistance because new arrivals cannot qualify for aid with less than one year of residence. Have other inmigrants come to Los Angeles to get on welfare rolls or rather to find job opportunities? I am sure that statistics bear out my observation rather than that which appears in the report.

2. I do not believe it is the function of this Commission to put a lid on protest registered by those sweltering in ghettos of the urban areas of our country. We speak of the malaise in our cities and in our society in general. We also recognize in our report that "The Negro found that he entered the competitive life of the city with very real handicaps: he lacked education, training, and experience, and his handicaps were aggravated by racial barriers which were more traditional than legal. He found himself, for reasons for which he had no responsibility and over which he had no control, in a situation in which providing a livelihood for himself and his family was most difficult and at times desperate. Thus, with the passage of time, altogether too often the rural Negro who has come to the city sinks into despair." Yet the report concludes that all of the ameliorating efforts — such as education and other governmental programs — will be of no avail unless he helps himself. It is true that you cannot make a musician out of a child who is unwilling to learn, even though you provide the best teachers and the best instruments. But it must be remembered in

dealing with the member of a disadvantaged minority who has never heard music or seen a musical instrument that he must be motivated to help himself. Therefore, he has a right to protest when circumstances do not allow him to participate in the mainstream of American society. Protest against forces which reduce individuals to second-class citizens, political, cultural, and psychological nonentities, are part of the celebrated American tradition. As long as an individual "stands outside looking in" he is not part of that society; that society cannot say that he does not have a right to protest, nor can it say that he must shoulder a responsibility which he has never been given an opportunity to assume.

APPENDIX

STAFF

GOVERNOR'S COMMISSION
ON THE LOS ANGELES RIOTS

Thomas R. Sheridan
General Counsel and Executive Director

Harold W. Horowitz
Deputy General Counsel

Community Liaison
C. Joseph Bride, Jr.

Program Manager
Marvin Adelson

Staff Attorneys
Yvonne Brathwaite
Alice Campbell
Benjamin S. Farber
John A. Joannes
John A. Mitchell
Kevin O'Connell
Gerald L. Rosen
James S. White
Samuel L. Williams

Staff Investigators
Logan Lane, *Chief*
Alfred V. Branche
David A. Butterfield
William W. Colby
Jerry Curtis
Loring D. Emile
William C. Gilkey
Kenneth V. Hansen
Malcolm P. Richards
Carl W. Wullschlager

Research Associates
Renée A. Copes
William K. Salstrom

Research Assistants
Justine McCarthy
Judith R. Nelson
Audrey Oliver

Terence M. Lee
Secretary to the Commission

CONSULTANTS TO THE COMMISSION

Norman Abrams, Professor of Law, University of California, Los Angeles

James N. Adler, Attorney at Law

Robert Blauner, Assistant Professor of Sociology, University of California, Berkeley

John C. Bollens, Professor of Political Science, University of California, Los Angeles

Joseph Boskin, Associate Professor of History, University of Southern California

Paul Bullock, Research Economist, University of California, Los Angeles

Francis M. Carney, Associate Professor of Political Science, University of California, Riverside

Fred E. Case, Professor of Business Administration, University of California, Los Angeles

John M. Chapman, Professor of Epidemiology, University of California, Los Angeles

Michael E. DePrano, Assistant Professor of Economics, University of Southern California

Betty M. Edmundson, Psychiatric Social Worker, County General Hospital, Los Angeles

Frances L. Feldman, Associate Professor of Social Work, University of Southern California

M. Michael Feuers, Sociologist, System Development Corporation

Walter A. Fogel, Assistant Professor of Business Administration, University of California, Los Angeles

Maxwell E. Greenberg, Attorney at Law

Kent M. Lloyd, Assistant Professor of Public Administration, University of Southern California

Kenneth A. Martyn, Professor of Special Education, California State College at Los Angeles

Jeffrey B. Nugent, Assistant Professor of Economics, University of Southern California

E. Edward Ransford, Graduate Student, Department of Sociology, University of California, Los Angeles

Leo G. Reeder, Associate Professor of Public Health, University of California, Los Angeles

William L. Rivers, Associate Professor of Communication, Stanford University

Milton Roemer, Professor of Public Health, University of California, Los Angeles

Melvin Seeman, Professor of Sociology, University of California, Los Angeles

Harold W. Solomon, Associate Professor of Law, University of Southern California

Henry J. Steinman, Attorney at Law

Irwin R. Sternlicht, Clinical Psychologist, System Development Corporation

Clerical and Secretarial

Betty Barnett, *Secretary to Mr. McCone*

June Perkins, *Secretary to Mr. Sheridan*

Hank Ares

Nancy J. Bell

Carrie E. Blanchard

Joanne Burnside

Barbara Christiansen

Shirley Doyle

Chris Duda

Lucy Fidchina

Sue Heard

Martha Hubbard

Eleanor Navickas

Mary Stave

Lucy Woods

Nelson & Amack
Official Reporters

ALPHABETICAL LIST OF SWORN WITNESSES

Anderson, Glenn M.	Lieutenant Governor, State of California
Atkinson, Herb	Vice-President, Atkinson Transportation Co. and South Los Angeles Transportation Co.
Billett, John W.	Administrative Assistant to the Executive Secretary to the Governor, State of California
Bradley, Thomas	Councilman, 10th District, City of Los Angeles
Brazier, Wesley R.	Executive Director, Los Angeles Urban League
Brookins, Reverend H. Hartford	Chairman, United Civil Rights Committee and Pastor, First AME Church of Los Angeles
Brown, Edmund G.	Governor, State of California
Brown, Willie F.	Resident of Compton since 1940
Brunton, George E.	Division Fire Chief, Fire Department, County of Los Angeles
Bryant, Miss Linda	Student, David Starr Jordan High School in Watts, President of Student Committee for Improvement in Watts
Buggs, John A.	Executor Director, Los Angeles County Commission on Human Relations

Champion, Hale	Director, Department of Finance, State of California
Christian, Winslow	Executive Secretary to the Governor, State of California
Claybrook, Harvey	Accountant, formerly employed at Martin's Department Store, in Watts
Collins, Wendell	First Vice-Chairman, Congress of Racial Equality
Colwell, Capt. Walter C.	Commander, Internal Affairs Division, Department of Police, City of Los Angeles
Cray, Ed	Representative of the American Civil Liberties Union of Southern California
Crittenden, Bradford	Administrator, Public Safety Agency and Commissioner, California Highway Patrol
Crowther, Jack P.	Superintendent of Los Angeles City School District
Dorn, Warren M.	Supervisor, 5th District, Los Angeles County
Downey, James F.	Undersheriff, Sheriff's Department, County of Los Angeles
Dymally, Mervyn M.	Assemblyman, 53rd District, State of California

Eberhardt, Jack L.	Sergeant, Manuals and Order Section of Planning and Research Division, Department of Police, City of Los Angeles
Ferraro, John	President, Board of Police Commissioners, City of Los Angeles
Fisher, Hugo	Administrator, Resources Agency, State of California
Fisk, James G.	Administrative Inspector, and Coordinator of Community Relations Activities, Department of Police, City of Los Angeles
Forniss, Mrs. Mary Ann	Resident of Watts
Gibson, John S. Jr.	Councilman, 15th District, City of Los Angeles
Gonzaque, Mrs. Ozie	Watts resident for 22 years
Gordon, Milton G.	Real Estate Commissioner and Administrator, Business and Commerce Agency, State of California
Gregg, Mrs. Jean	Executive Director, Crenshaw Neighbors, Inc.
Guzman, Ralph	Assistant Director, Mexican-American Study Project, University of California at Los Angeles

Haas, Lucien C.	Associate Press Secretary to the Governor, State of California
Hahn, Kenneth	Supervisor, 2nd District, County of Los Angeles
Hawkins, Augustus F.	Congressman, 21st Congressional District, State of California
Hill, Raymond M.	Administrative Deputy Chief, Los Angeles Fire Department
Hill, Lt. General Roderic L.	Adjutant General, State of California and Commander, California National Guard
Houston, Norman B.	President, Los Angeles Branch of the National Association for the Advancement of Colored People
Ingram, William K.	Chief of Police, Compton, California
Jasich, Antone P.	Captain, Arson Bureau, Los Angeles Fire Department
Johnson, Mrs. Freita Shaw	President, Will Frandel Ladies Club of Watts
Jones, Mrs. Opal C.	Director, Neighborhood Adult Participation Project
Kline, Richard	Staff Secretary to Governor Brown for Southern California

Lewis, Murray A.	Secretary, Management Committee, Los Angeles Chamber of Commerce
Lynch, Thomas C.	Attorney General, State of California
McClellan, H. C.	Chairman, Rehabilitation Committee, Los Angeles Chamber of Commerce
Maldonado, Joe P.	Executive Director, Economic and Youth Opportunities Agency of Greater Los Angeles
Miller, Loren	Judge, Los Angeles Municipal Courts; Vice-President, National Committee Against Discrimination in Housing
Mills, Billy G.	Councilman, 8th District, City of Los Angeles
Monning, Major General John C.	General Manager and Superintendent of Building, Department of Building and Safety, City of Los Angeles
Monroe, Eason	Executive Director, American Civil Liberties Union of Southern California
Mont, Max	Assistant to the Executive-Secretary-Treasurer of the Los Angeles County Federation of Labor, AFL-CIO

Morse, Mrs. Muriel M.	General Manager, Civil Service Department, City of Los Angeles
Muntz, Harold R.	Chief Deputy Probation Officer, Probation Department, County of Los Angeles
Murdock, Roger E.	Deputy Chief of Police Commander, Patrol Bureau, Department of Police, City of Los Angeles
Murphy, Ellis P.	Director, Bureau of Public Assistance, Department of Charities, County of Los Angeles
Nelson, Mrs. Helen	Consumer Counsel, State of California
Ott, Major General Charles A. Jr.	Commanding General of the 40th Armored Division, California National Guard
Parker, William H.	Chief of Police, Department of Police, City of Los Angeles
Peery, Benjamin	Long-time resident of Watts
Pitchess, Peter J.	Sheriff, Los Angeles County
Purnell, Eugene	Secretary of Anti-Poverty Committee, Hodcarriers Union, Local 300

Quick, Colonel Robert L.	Colonel, California National Guard
Reddin, Thomas	Deputy Chief of Police Commander, Technical Services Bureau, Department of Police, City of Los Angeles
Roybal, Edward R.	Congressman, 30th District, State of California
Rubin, Miles	Senior Assistant Attorney General, State of California
Schrade, Paul	Director, Western Region 6, United Auto Workers, AFL-CIO
Simon, Richard	Deputy Chief of Police Commander, Bureau of Administration, Department of Police, City of Los Angeles
Slaff, George	President, American Civil Liberties Union of Southern California
Slaughter, Winston	Compton Junior College Student
Taylor, Dr. Christopher L.	Dentist and property owner in riot area
Ward, Paul D.	Administrator, Health and Welfare Agency, State of California
Warren, Edward	Real estate broker in Watts area

Welch, Miss Sue	Former schoolteacher at Markham Junior High School in Watts
Williams, Mrs. Annabelle	Coordinator of Imperial Gardens Housing Project in Watts
Wing, Philip	Athletic Director, Verbum Dei High School in Watts
Wirin, A. L.	Counsel for American Civil Liberties Union of Southern California
Younger, Evelle J.	District Attorney, County of Los Angeles
Yorty, Samuel William	Mayor, City of Los Angeles

In addition to the above list of sworn witnesses, the Commission's staff conducted detailed interviews of several hundred witnesses, not only in Los Angeles, but also in other cities throughout the United States, such as Chicago, New Haven, Rochester, Philadelphia, New York, and Washington, D. C. The staff also interviewed some 90 persons arrested during the riots. Further, the Commission's consultants questioned many people and conducted written surveys of some 10,000 persons. The members of the Commission were given detailed reports of the interviews and studies.

The Commission opened and staffed three field offices in South Central Los Angeles where hundreds of local residents and business people were interviewed. Each Commissioner spent many hours in the field offices, and their interviews were written up and furnished to all other Commissioners.

The Commission wishes to acknowledge its debt and express its appreciation to all who so generously shared their knowledge, counsel, and observations with the Commission during its investigation.

WHITE ON BLACK:

A CRITIQUE OF THE McCONE COMMISSION

REPORT ON THE LOS ANGELES RIOTS

White on Black: A Critique of the McCone Commission Report on the Los Angeles Riots

ROBERT M. FOGELSON

Columbia University

The Los Angeles riots erupted on August 11, 1965, after a white California highway patrolman arrested a young Negro for drunken driving in the southcentral ghetto known as Watts. A scuffle involving the youth, his mother, and the patrol- man ensued, attracting a large crowd which was further incited by the arrival of the Los Angeles police. From about eight that evening to one the next morning, mobs stoned passing automo- biles, assaulted white motorists, and threatened a police command post. On August 12 after a tumultuous meeting called by the Los Angeles County Human Relations Commission, the rioting, ac- companied by looting and arson, spread throughout the ghetto. At great personal risk many Negro leaders, some from Los Angeles and others of national renown, pleaded with the rioters to end the violence, but to little or no avail. The next day the disorder was so widespread that Los Angeles Police Chief William Parker asked California Lieutenant Governor Glenn Anderson (standing in for vacationing Governor Edmund Brown) to order in the National Guard. Guardsmen and rioters besieged Watts that evening, and after Anderson imposed a curfew the authorities slowly suppressed the nation's worst race riots in a generation. On August 15—with 34 persons dead, over 1,000 injured, and almost 4,000 arrested,

600 buildings damaged and $20-40 million in property destroyed —the ghetto was pacified.[1]

Four days later Governor Brown (by then returned to California) appointed a commission consisting of six whites and two Negroes and headed by John A. McCone, a prominent industrialist and former director of the CIA, to make "an objective and dispassionate study of the Los Angeles riots." Brown instructed the commission to "prepare an accurate chronology and description of the riots . . . probe deeply the immediate and underlying causes of the riots . . . [and] develop recommendations for action designed to prevent a recurrence of these tragic disorders." The commission, which was allocated $250,000, hired 29 staff members, 16 clerks and secretaries, and 26 consultants, and then launched its investigation. It heard 79 witnesses, including Governor Brown and his advisers, local politicians, police administrators, civil libertarians, teachers, Negro spokesmen, and Watts residents, its staff interviewed several hundred persons, including 90 arrested during the riots, and its consultants questioned another 10,000 people. Working at an extremely, perhaps unduly, rapid pace, the commission completed its investigation in three months. And on December 2, 1965, it presented its interpretations of the riots and its recommendations for public policy in an eighty-six page report entitled "Violence in the City—an End or a Beginning?"[2]

Put bluntly, "Violence in the City" claimed that the rioters were marginal people and the riots meaningless outbursts. The rioters were marginal people, according to the McCone Commission, because they were a small and unrepresentative fraction of the Negro population, namely, the unemployed, ill-educated, juvenile, delinquent, and uprooted. What provoked them to riot were not conditions endemic to Negro ghettos (police harassment and consumer exploitation), but rather problems peculiar to immigrant groups (resentment of police, insufficient skills, and inferior education) and irresponsible agitation by Negro leaders. Also, the riots were

[1] Jerry Cohen and William S. Murphy, *Burn, Baby, Burn! The Los Angeles Race Riot, August, 1965* (New York, 1966), 78-222; Governor's Commission on the Los Angeles Riots, *Archives*, II, in the University of California Library, Los Angeles (hereafter referred to as *MCA*).

[2] *Violence in the City—An End or a Beginning? A Report by the Governor's Commission on the Los Angeles Riots* (Dec. 2, 1965), (hereafter referred to as *MCR*). For Governor Brown's charge, see *ibid.*, i-iii.

meaningless outbursts, according to the McCone Commission, not simply because there was no connection between the Negroes' grievances and their violence, but also because the rioting was unwarranted. Watts, for all its inadequacies, is not, like Harlem, a slum—its streets are wide and clean, and its houses are detached one- and two-story dwellings; nor are its residents, like Southern Negroes, subject to racial discrimination—to the contrary, they enjoy full legal and political equality.[3] Thus, to prevent a repetition of rioting in southcentral Los Angeles, "Violence in the City" concluded, requires that police-civilian relations be improved, unemployment reduced, education upgraded, and civil rights protests suppressed.

Less than two months later the California Advisory Committee to the United States Civil Rights Commission challenged the McCone Commission's findings and recommendations. Shortly thereafter Bayard Rustin, the well-known civil rights spokesman, Robert Blauner, a Berkeley sociologist, and Harry Scoble, a U.C.L.A. political scientist, criticized the report, too.[4] Notwithstanding a few differences, these critics agreed on the following crucial points. First, that a much larger and more representative segment of the ghetto populace than the McCone Commission estimated joined the rioting and that many others who did not participate supported the rioters. Second, that the Negroes rioted because they could not passively accept conditions in the ghetto any longer and not because they were unprepared for urban life or because their leaders were contemptuous of law and order. Third, that the rioting, and especially the looting and burning, were articulate protests against genuine grievances and, as such, meaningful protests against the southcentral ghetto. Fourth, that the Watts vicinity is, by any physical or psychological criteria, a slum, in which Los Angeles' Negroes are rigorously and involuntarily segregated.

[3] *Ibid.*, 2-9 and *passim.*
[4] California Advisory Committee to the United States Commission on Civil Rights, "An Analysis of the McCone Commission Report" (Jan. 1966); Bayard Rustin, "The Watts 'Manifesto' and the McCone Report," *Commentary*, XLI (1966), 29-35; Robert Blauner, "Whitewash Over Watts," *Trans-action*, III (1966), 3 ff; Harry M. Scoble, "The McCone Commission and Social Science" (Aug. 1966), unpublished paper written for the U.S. Office of Economic Opportunity.

Hence, to maintain public order in Los Angeles, these critics countered, demands fundamental changes not only in the Negro ghetto but in the white metropolis as well.

The controversy between the McCone Commission and its critics was resolved late in 1966 when the U.C.L.A. Institute of Government and Public Affairs completed a survey of the Los Angeles riots for the U.S. Office of Economic Opportunity, and I finished a report on the riots of the nineteen-sixties for the President's Commission on Law Enforcement and Administration of Justice.[5] Together, these studies left little doubt that the McCone Commission completely misunderstood the character and implications of the Los Angeles riots. Yet, as the McCone Commission archives were inaccessible for several months after the investigation, none of the critics (nor, for other reasons, either of the studies) made it clear just why the commission failed. Accordingly, it was not until the summer of 1966, when these archives—which consist of the report, a chronology of the rioting, twelve volumes of formal hearings by the commission, two volumes of informal interviews by its staff, and two volumes of consultants' papers—were deposited in the California State Library in Sacramento and the University of California Library in Los Angeles, that it was possible to reconstruct the McCone Commission investigation and to discern where and why it went wrong.

The McCone Commission archives indicate that the investigation failed for more profound reasons than the critics presumed. To begin with, the most obvious explanation offered, that the commission was unduly hasty in its work, is true but hardly crucial. This is not to deny that the commission's schedule—which allowed only slightly more than three months for the investigation[6]—was exceedingly tight and its pace excessively rapid. Nor is it to deny that the commission presented an extremely sketchy report, a document much less impressive than the exhaustive study of the Chicago riots of 1919 and even the modest account of the

[5] Robert M. Fogelson, "The 1960's Riots: Interpretations and Recommendations," a report prepared for the President's Commission on Law Enforcement and Administration of Justice, December 1966. The Institute's study is presently being prepared for publication under the supervision of Professor Nat Cohen who kindly allowed me to read the preliminary findings.
[6] Blauner, 3.

Harlem riots of 1935.[7] It is rather to claim that during the three months available, as a careful reading of the report, hearings, interviews, and consultants' papers reveals, the McCone Commission collected enough information for a satisfactory, though not definitive, explanation of the 1965 rioting. And so completely did the commissioners ignore or misinterpret this information that there is no reason to believe that if given three years rather than three months they would have prepared a better report.

The critics also contended that the McCone Commission was not inclined to probe deeply into the Los Angeles riots anyway.[8] There is much to support this assertion. Governor Brown, who was gravely concerned about his political future (with good cause, it turned out), well knew that the riots were an explosive issue. Hence he appointed an impeccably conservative commission. In addition to McCone, who, by virtue of his prestige, dominated the deliberations, it consisted of a prominent attorney, the chairman of the Pacific Mutual Life Insurance Company, the president of Loyola University, the dean of the U.C.L.A. Medical School, and a former president of the California League of Women Voters (the six whites) as well as a municipal judge and a Presbyterian pastor (the two Negroes). Except for the two Negroes, who were anything but militant and exerted little influence over the commission, the commissioners were representative of California's establishment. This was hardly auspicious because blue-ribbon commissions in the United States, unlike royal commissions in Great Britain, have as a rule sought political, as opposed to literal, truth.[9] And the McCone Commission was no exception.

There is, however, a more crucial explanation for the McCone Commission's failure. The commissioners were not altogether unsympathetic to the plight of Negroes in the southcentral ghetto, nor were they unintelligent or irresponsible. They were, to the con-

[7] Chicago Commission on Race Relations, The Negro in Chicago: A Study of Race Relations and a Race Riot (Chicago, 1922); Mayor's Commission on Conditions in Harlem, "The Negro in Harlem: A Report on Social and Economic Conditions Responsible for the Outbreak of March 19, 1935" (New York, 1936).
[8] Rustin, 33-34; Blauner, 2-3.
[9] Charles J. Hanser, Guide to Decision: The Royal Commission (Tottowa, N.J., 1965), especially Chap. 10.

trary, representative of upper-middle-class whites in Los Angeles and other American cities. Accordingly, they brought to their task assorted preconceptions about violence, law enforcement, ghettos, and slums, preconceptions which they shared with others of their class and race. These preconceptions—they emerge clearly from the hearings and, less so, from the report—prevented the commission from perceptively analyzing the evidence and correctly interpreting the riots. For they filtered the testimony and other information received by the commissioners and enabled them to draw conclusions based on the flimsiest material while ignoring more substantial but less reassuring data. Hence, a reconsideration of the investigation is worthwhile not only because "Violence in the City" is the fullest official statement about any riots of the nineteen-sixties, but also because the McCone Commission's fiasco sharply illuminates why most white Americans have thus far failed to understand the Negro riots.

I

At the outset of the investigation the McCone Commission reached the conclusion that only 10,000, or approximately two per cent, of Los Angeles County's 650,000 Negroes joined the rioting. Moreover, it contended, the rioters were not representative of the Negro community; they were the unemployed, ill-educated, delinquent, juvenile, and uprooted—in short, the riffraff.[10] The overwhelming majority of Los Angeles' Negroes, the commission implied, were law-abiding, that is, non-riotous; doubtless they, like Los Angeles' whites, disapproved of the disturbances. The riffraff theory, it should be noted, was not formulated for the first time by the McCone Commission. It had been adopted a year earlier by Paul Screvane, acting mayor of New York City, and Nelson Rockefeller, governor of New York State, in order to explain the Harlem, Bedford-Stuyvesant, and Rochester riots.[11] Nevertheless, for the McCone Commission (as well as for the Brown administration and California's white majority), the conclusion that the Negro riffraff

[10] MCA, III, Testimony of Lieutenant Governor Glenn M. Anderson, 22; MCR, 1, 3, 5, 24.
[11] New York *Times*, July 22, Aug. 4, 1964; Newark *Evening News*, July 20, 1964; New York *Journal-American*, July 26, 1964.

was primarily responsible for the Los Angeles riots was reassuring indeed.

If the rioters were only a small group of unemployed, ill-edu-. cated, delinquent, juvenile, and uprooted Negroes then the Los Angeles riots were less serious than the concern they aroused indicated. It follows that the rioting was not only peripheral to the issue of Negro-white relations, but also a manifestation of problems of poverty, which, in American thought, is alterable, rather than race, which is, by contrast, immutable. It also follows that the Los Angeles riots reflected not so much the social problems inherent in modern Negro ghettos as the personal disabilities of recent Negro newcomers. It follows further that the violent acts, the assaults, arson, and theft, were not expressions of legitimate grievances and that they were, in the words of the McCone Commission, "formless, quite senseless," and, by implication, meaningless.[12] Hence future riots could be prevented in southcentral Los Angeles merely by elevating the riffraff without transforming the Negro ghetto—without, in effect, radically changing greater Los Angeles or seriously inconveniencing its white majority.

Given the profound implications of the riffraff theory, its foundations should have been based on solid evidence. Yet little evidence, solid or otherwise, is contained in "Violence in the City." For all its hearings, interviews, and consultants, the McCone Commission made no surveys of riot participation. Instead, it derived its estimate that only two per cent of Los Angeles' Negroes joined in the riots from the impressions of Mayor Samuel Yorty, Police Chief Parker, and other officials who had good reason to minimize the extent of participation.[13] Furthermore, the commission based its conclusion that the rioters were the riffraff on nothing more than a statistical survey of the persons arrested during the rioting according to age, prior criminal record, and place of birth. It did not present the comparable statistics for southcentral Los Angeles which would have revealed that the number of juveniles, criminals, and newcomers involved was not, in fact, disproportionately

[12] MCR, 4-5.
[13] MCA, III, Testimony of Lieutenant Governor Glenn Anderson, 22-23; XI, Testimony of Police Chief William H. Parker, 87-89; XIV, Testimony of Mayor Samuel W. Yorty, 58-61.

high.[14] Nor did it compile any data about the employment rates and educational levels of the rioters. Finally, the commission offered no proof that the great majority of Los Angeles' Negroes disapproved of the rioting, and even ignored the testimony of many middle-class Negroes who did not riot but admitted that they fully sympathized with the rioters.[15]

Why, then, in the absence of corroborating evidence, did the McCone Commission adopt the riffraff theory? The answer, I believe, can be traced to its conviction that no matter how grave the grievances, there are no legitimate grounds for violent protest—a conviction, shared by most whites and, until recently, most Negroes, which reflects the nation's traditional confidence in orderly social change.[16] To have accepted—indeed, even to have raised—the possibility that a substantial and representative segment of Los Angeles' Negroes participated in the riots would have compelled the commission to draw either of two conclusions: one, that the deterioration of the southcentral ghetto has destroyed the prospect for gradual progress and provided the justification for violent protest; the other, that even if the commission does not believe that the situation is anywhere so desperate, a large number of ordinary Negroes in Los Angeles does not agree with it. Neither conclusion could have been reconciled with the commission's commitment to orderly, and extremely limited, social change. And to have accepted either would have obliged the commissioners to re-examine a fundamental feature of the ideology of their class, race, and country. Not surprisingly, they, like most of their countrymen, were not inclined to do so.

The riffraff theory is wrong, however. On the basis of statistical

[14] For these figures, see Bureau of Criminal Statistics, California Department of Justice, "Summary of a Preliminary Report of Persons Arrested in the Los Angeles Riots" (Nov. 1965), ibid., II; MCR, 24; U.S. Bureau of the Census, Current Population Reports, Series P-23, No. 18, "Characteristics of the South and East Los Angeles Areas: November 1965" (Washington, D.C., 1966), 38; idem, United States Census of Population: 1960. Detailed Characteristics. California. Final Report (Washington, D.C., 1962), 478, 485; The President's Commission on Law Enforcement and Administration of Justice, The Challenge of Crime in a Free Society (Washington, D.C., 1967), 75.

[15] MCA, XV, Interview 29; XVI, Interview 90.

[16] MCR, 6-7. See, also, Louis Hartz, The Liberal Tradition in America (New York, 1955), Chap. I; Gresham M. Sykes, Crime and Society (New York, 1966), 79.

and other data now available, the McCone Commission's estimate that only 10,000, or approximately two per cent, of Los Angeles County's 650,000 Negroes participated in the riots is wholly far-fetched. For to claim that only 10,000 Negroes rioted when almost 4,000 were arrested is to presume that the police apprehended fully forty per cent of the rioters, a presumption which, as Harry Scoble has pointed out, is inconsistent with all the descriptions of the rioting.[17] Indeed, recent surveys conducted by David O. Sears, a U.C.L.A. political scientist, and John F. Kraft, Inc., an opinion research organization, reveal that the figure is at least 30,000 and perhaps even as high as 80,000.[18] Of the 650,000 Negroes then living in Los Angeles County, moreover, no more than 450,000 resided in the curfew area; and of these, roughly 180,000—nearly all children under twelve and adults over sixty—did not participate in the rioting.[19] Thus, of the potential rioters, the male and female adolescents and young and middle-age adults—and the McCone Commission notwithstanding, potential rioters, not total population, is the appropriate base on which to compute riot participation —a substantial minority, at the very least, joined in the 1965 riots.

Arrest data and survey research also refute the McCone Commission's conclusion that the rioters were the unemployed, ill-educated, delinquent, juvenile, and uprooted, and they alone. The commission's profile is not only internally inconsistent—in Los Angeles, a study prepared for the Area Redevelopment Administration by the U.C.L.A. Institute of Industrial Relations reveals, the newcomers tend to be better educated and more regularly employed than the older residents[20]—but, in addition, it does not accurately describe the rioters. Young adults and not minors made up the large majority of the arrestees; that most of them had prior

[17] Scoble, "The McCone Commission," 11.
[18] John F. Kraft, Inc., "Attitudes of Negroes in Various Cities," a report prepared for the U.S. Senate Subcommittee on Executive Reorganization ([New York], 1966), 5-6; David O. Sears, "Riot Activity and Evaluation: An Overview of the Negro Survey" (1966), 1-2, unpublished paper written for the U.S. Office of Economic Opportunity.
[19] U.S. Bureau of the Census, "Characteristics of the South and East Los Angeles Areas," 38.
[20] Institute of Industrial Relations, University of California, Los Angeles, "Hard-Core Unemployment and Poverty in Los Angeles" (Washington, D.C., 1965), 143-45.

records reflects not so much their criminality as the high incidence of arrest in the ghetto. Evidence about educational achievement suggests that the rioters were, if anything, slightly better educated than their peers; so, U.C.L.A. survey research indicates, were their parents. And data on employment and residence, also based on arrest records, show that the great majority of the rioters had lived in Los Angeles for at least five years and were currently employed. For these reasons the U.C.L.A. Institute of Government and Public Affairs study of riot participation concluded that the Los Angeles rioters were very much in "the mainstream of modern Negro urban life."[21]

The recent surveys of public opinion in the southcentral ghetto also contradict the McCone Commission's implication that an overwhelming proportion of Los Angeles' Negroes disapproved of the riots. Not only did a substantial and representative minority actually participate in the rioting, but, in addition, many others who did not riot sympathized with the rioters.[22] Nor did attitudes in the ghetto change later. Whereas a small majority of Negroes interviewed after the rioting expressed confidence in non-violence, nearly as many believed that the riots had improved the position of their race. Also, many who disapproved of the rioting gave as their reason the fact that Negroes, not whites, suffered the brunt of the casualties—the personal injuries as opposed to the property losses. Asked what impact the riots had on them as Negroes, a slight majority answered that they felt more pride, a large minority reported no change, and almost none said that they felt less pride.[23] Contrary to the McCone Commission's findings, then, the Los Angeles riots were made by a large minority of the potential rioters, typical of the young adult Negro population, which received widespread support within the ghetto.

This conclusion has very different, but no less profound, implications than the riffraff theory. If the rioters were a substantial and representative minority, sympathetically regarded by the

[21] Sears, 1-13; Los Angeles County Probation Department, "Riot Participation Study: Juvenile Offenders" (Nov. 1965); Bureau of Criminal Statistics, California Department of Criminal Justice, "Watts Riots Arrests: Los Angeles August 1965" (June 30, 1966).
[22] MCA, XVI, Interview 90.
[23] John F. Kraft, Inc., "Attitudes of Negroes," 4, 6, 7; Sears, 5-6.

Negro community, then the Los Angeles riots were clearly of the utmost importance. They were not only central to the issue of Negro-white relations, but also manifestations of problems of race even more than class. Indeed, there is considerable evidence that working- and middle-class Negroes resent the indignities of ghetto life more than lower-class Negroes do. The rioting also reflected social problems endemic to Negro ghettos rather than personal disabilities peculiar to immigrant groups—or, as Bayard Rustin put it, the unpreparedness not of the newcomers, but of the cities. And the violent acts were expressions of genuine grievances and, as such, meaningful protests. If these implications are valid, moreover, future riots can be prevented only by transforming the southcentral ghetto, not simply by elevating the riffraff—a recommendation which is highly irresponsible and downright dangerous when exploited, as it was by the McCone Commission, to obscure the legitimate grievances of Los Angeles' Negroes.

II

The Los Angeles riots made it quite clear that many Negroes in the southcentral ghetto regard the conduct of the Los Angeles police as one of these grievances. The incident which precipitated the rioting—a commonplace and, were it not for what followed, trivial arrest for drunken driving—is otherwise incomprehensible. Why else did hundreds of Negroes gather at the site of the arrest— an arrest wholly justified and properly handled—shout abuse at the patrolmen, attempt to free the prisoners, and even hurl bricks at the police cars? Why else did so many Negroes believe the wild rumors that the patrolmen were mistreating other Negroes which swiftly spread through the ghetto? Why else did the arrival of police reinforcements attract a thousand or so Negroes to the scene and so incite them that the crowd was transformed into a mob? And why else did the rioters later vent their hostility against the Los Angeles patrolmen and not, with some exceptions, against the guardsmen?[24] So overwhelming is this evidence that even the McCone Commission realized that police action has an incendiary effect in the southcentral ghetto that it has nowhere else in Los

[24] MCR, 10-12; MCA, XII, Testimony of Benjamin Peery, a long-time Watts resident, 5-6; Cohen and Murphy, 50-59.

Angeles. And for this reason the commission spent many of its sessions investigating Negro resentment of police.

A host of middle-class Negro witnesses testified at these sessions that many Negroes are unduly resentful of the Los Angeles police because of their earlier experience with Southern policemen. Nonetheless, they insisted, even in Los Angeles, Negroes are victims of police brutality and police harassment so often that their resentment is justified. The Negro witnesses also conceded that for the patrolmen who work there (as for the people who live there) the southcentral ghetto is a very dangerous place. Even so, they pointed out, Negroes are convinced, and with good reason, that the police enforce the law less rigorously in their community than elsewhere in Los Angeles.[25] It is because, as Assemblyman Mervyn M. Dymally told the McCone Commission, Negroes have "generally expected the worst from the police and generally received it"[26] that they resent the police. To ease this resentment, Dymally and the other Negro witnesses urged the commission to recommend that brutality and harassment be eliminated, law enforcement tightened, and an independent police review board established.

The Los Angeles Police Department spokesmen, Chief Parker, John Ferraro, president of the Board of Police Commissioners, and Mayor Yorty, replied to the Negro witnesses. They insisted that their charges—according to Parker, manifestations of the dwindling respect for law and order in the United States and attempts to undermine the effectiveness of law enforcement in Los Angeles—were altogether unfounded. Police brutality is extremely uncommon, they argued, police harassment is deplored and discouraged, and a single standard of law enforcement is maintained everywhere in Los Angeles. The resentment of Negroes, they claimed, is due to their past mistreatment in the South and present maladjustment in the North, and not to the conduct of the police in the ghetto. Negroes vent their hostility toward patrolmen not as

[25] MCA, III, Testimony of Councilman Thomas Bradley, 29-36; V, Testimony of John A. Buggs, executive director of the Los Angeles County Human Relations Commission, 18-23; VI, Testimony of Assemblyman Mervyn M. Dymally, 48-49; VIII, Testimony of Congressman Augustus F. Hawkins, 82-85; X, Testimony of Councilman Billy G. Mills, 9-10.

[26] Mervyn M. Dymally, "Statement Prepared for the Governor's Commission on the Los Angeles Riots" (Oct. 11, 1965), 2.

patrolmen, but as representatives of white society and white authority; the police are the recipients, not the source, of Negro resentment. Past practices aside, the police department's spokesmen assured the McCone Commission, Los Angeles' Negroes have no genuine grievances against the police, and thus no major departmental reforms are necessary.[27]

The McCone Commission largely endorsed the police department's position.[28] It ignored the allegations of inadequate law enforcement, dismissed the charges of brutality and harassment, and concluded that the problem of Negro-police relations was a problem not of misconduct but of misunderstanding of the police by Negroes and of Negroes by the police. To alleviate this misunderstanding, the commission recommended that the police department's procedure for handling civilian complaints be revised, but it rejected Negro demands for an independent police review board —on the grounds that such boards have not worked well in two other cities (both of which were unnamed) and that they tend to demoralize patrolmen (though Negro, not police, morale was the issue here)—and proposed instead the creation of an "inspector general" under the jurisdiction of the chief of police. It also recommended the professionalization of the Board of Police Commissioners, the non-salaried citizens agency which has ultimate responsibility for the police force, and the expansion of the police department's current, though ineffective, community relations program.[29]

To reach these conclusions was no mean task. The McCone Commission had to do more than merely reject the testimony of its middle-class Negro witnesses. It also had to disregard the affidavits and other evidence submitted by the southern California chapter of the American Civil Liberties Union substantiating the allegations of police misconduct and to ignore the statement of one Los Angeles policeman who reluctantly admitted that most white patrolmen simply cannot distinguish between law-abiding and

[27] MCA, VI, Testimony of John Ferraro, president of the Los Angeles Board of Police Commissioners, 5-8; XI, Testimony of Police Chief William Parker, 3-36; XIV, Testimony of Mayor Samuel W. Yorty, 58-61.
[28] MCR, 27-28.
[29] Ibid., 29-37.

lawless colored people.[80] Finally, it had to accept unqualifiedly the testimony of Chief Parker, a man whose antipathy to the civil rights movement was exceeded only by his devotion to the Los Angeles police, whose professional views were extremely conservative even for an extremely conservative profession, and whose personal behavior at the commission's hearings bordered, I believe, on the paranoid.[81] The McCone Commission had to overcome all these seemingly insuperable obstacles without the benefit of any surveys or other data refuting the Negroes' complaints or supporting the police department's replies. That it—or, more accurately, Chairman McCone, for the other commissioners deferred to him in the examination of the problem of Negro-police relations—did so nonetheless is indeed remarkable.

What is even more remarkable is that McCone had already resolved this problem by the start of the investigation. Questioning George Slaff of the American Civil Liberties Union—to whom he was inexcusably rude[32]—McCone remarked that as CIA director he learned that in all the recent American riots and overseas insurrections the issue of police brutality was raised in order to destroy effective law enforcement. This tactic is reprehensible, he explained, because society is held together by respect for law, and respect for law is maintained by effective law enforcement, an assertion which reappeared almost verbatim in "Violence in the City,"[33] even though Slaff and others challenged its fundamental premise at the hearings. If police brutality is admitted, McCone reasoned, police authority will be undermined, law will be disregarded, society will be disrupted, and, in the words of the report, "chaos might easily result"—a prospect for which the commission was unwilling to assume any responsibility. That effective law en-

[80] MCA, XIII, Testimony of Richard Simon, Los Angeles Police Department, 8-9; Testimony of George Slaff, American Civil Liberties Union, 9-12.
[81] For indications of Parker's paranoia, see ibid., XI, Testimony of Police Chief William H. Parker, 16, 37-38, 119, and especially 121, where he claimed that Negro leaders "seem to think that if Parker can be destroyed officially, then they will have no more trouble in imposing their will upon the police of America, and that's about what it amounts to, because nobody else will dare stand up."
[32] Ibid., XIII, Testimony of George Slaff, American Civil Liberties Union, 9-11.
[33] See McCone's statement in ibid., 26-27, and the commission's position in MCR, 28-29.

forcement is only one among many sources of respect for law, that respect for law is only one among many supports of public order, and, indeed, that society is not simply a collection of predatory individuals and groups, McCone did not realize. Given his preconceptions and the other commissioners' deference, then, the commission could not have reached any other conclusions.

These conclusions are untenable, however, because they are inconsistent with the testimony and evidence offered by Negro witnesses and Civil Liberties Union spokesmen, and, more vital, because they are contradicted by two independent surveys of police conduct in the southcentral ghetto subsequently prepared by the Kraft organization and U.C.L.A. psychologist Walter J. Raine. These surveys reveal that most Los Angeles Negroes, middle class as well as lower class and law-abiding as well as lawless, have suffered police brutality or police harassment at one time or another.[84] These surveys also indicate that few Negroes in the southcentral ghetto believe that they receive adequate police protection, a belief which is supported by the crime statistics Chief Parker submitted to the McCone Commission. Hence, without analyzing the Negroes' complaints or the patrolmen's conduct at this point, it is still possible to define brutality, harassment, and inadequate protection as the primary problems which generate Negro resentment of the police in Los Angeles and which precipitated the riots in 1965.

The McCone Commission notwithstanding, these problems are problems of substance, not simply understanding, which the commission's recommendations do little to alleviate. Professionalization of the Board of Police Commissioners is irrelevant because it is not intrinsically related to the questions of brutality, harassment, and inadequate police protection in the ghetto. Establishment of an "inspector general"—as opposed to an independent civilian review board—is valueless because the Negroes will not place their trust in any police official, no matter how impressive

[84] John F. Kraft, Inc., "Attitudes of Negroes," 12-14, 23-25; Walter J. Raine, "The Perception of Police Brutality in South Central Los Angeles Following the Revolt of August 1965" (1966), 2-12, unpublished study prepared for the U.S. Office of Economic Opportunity; California Advisory Committee to the United States Commission on Civil Rights, "Report on California: Police-Minority Group Relations" (Aug. 1963), 7-31.

his title. And expansion of the police department's community relations program is at best moderately beneficial and at worst, if exploited, as it was by the McCone Commission, to avoid the real issue, dangerously misguided. That issue is to provide southcentral Los Angeles with the same law enforcement as the rest of the metropolis, a policy which would reduce brutality and harassment and at the same time enhance police protection. This is not, politically or otherwise, a simple task. But if the relationship between police and Negroes in Los Angeles is to be improved so that commonplace incidents do not trigger terrible confrontations, it is absolutely imperative.

III

The McCone Commission did not do much better in its investigation of the other reasons underlying the 1965 riots. That there were other reasons no one, not the commission and not its critics, seriously doubted. After all, though only a thousand Negroes gathered at the scene of the triggering incident, thousands more, few of whom had witnessed the initial arrest, subsequently joined in the rioting. Night after night, for almost a week, they left their homes and, with a camaraderie and enthusiasm usually reserved for festive occasions, thronged the streets. There they not only attacked patrolmen (flinging bricks and Molotov cocktails and firing rifles from the rooftops), but also assaulted white passers-by and looted and burned neighborhood stores.[35] By these actions a minor disturbance developed into a full-scale riot. This development was not inevitable; there are too many instances in which bands of Americans, often adolescent members of ethnic minorities, challenged police authority without provoking widespread disorder for this to be so.[36] But neither was it accidental. It was rather a violent manifestation of the fact that the Negroes in Los Angeles resent several other conditions in the southcentral ghetto just as keenly as they resent police misconduct. To define these conditions, and to recommend action to remedy them, was the McCone Commission's principal responsibility.

[35] MCR, 12-20; MCA, II, passim; XVI, Interview 29; Cohen and Murphy, 85-175.
[36] Harrison Salisbury, The Shook-Up Generation (New York, 1958), Chaps. 2, 5, 6, 11.

To this end the commission received from its witnesses and consultants sixteen volumes of testimony and reports which, for all its inconsistencies, made certain points quite clear. First, that in addition to police misconduct the crucial problems of Los Angeles' Negroes, and not only its lower-class Negroes, are economic deprivation, consumer exploitation, inadequate accommodations, and racial discrimination. Second, that these problems are deeply rooted in the conditions of ghetto life, especially in the high rates of unemployment, extreme risks of business enterprise, rigid patterns of residential segregation, and the profound weakness of Negro leadership. Third, that the Los Angeles rioters were so highly selective in their violence that, with few exceptions, they looted and burned only white-owned stores which charged outrageous prices, sold inferior goods, and applied extortionate credit arrangements.[37]

For the McCone Commission it was one thing to receive this information and quite another to accept it. A few examples should suffice to illustrate this difference. Jeffrey Nugent and Michael DePrano, University of Southern California economists, suggested that the rioting was generated by the disparity between the Negro's adequate educational achievements and his inadequate employment opportunities.[38] An imaginative hypothesis, but one incompatible with the riffraff theory, it was completely ignored by the commission. Paul Schrade, a United Automobile Workers Union official, argued that unemployment in the ghetto is due primarily to job shortages in greater Los Angeles, an assertion which contradicted the assumption that individual disabilities, not social conditions, provoked the rioting.[39] McCone sharply dissented, claiming that the problem is a function of insufficient training, and the commission adopted his position. Thomas Reddin, deputy chief of the Los Angeles Police Department, testified that the patterns of theft and arson in the riots revealed that the rioters vented

[37] Rustin, 29-30; Alex Rosen, "The Riots in Watts, Los Angeles," 7, paper presented at the 13th National Institute on Crime and Delinquency, Atlantic City, New Jersey, June 14, 1966; Fogelson, "The 1960's Riots," Chap. III.

[38] Michael E. DePrano and Jeffrey B. Nugent, "Economic Aspects of the L.A. Riots and Proposed Solutions," MCA, XVII.

[39] Ibid., XII, Testimony of Paul Schrade, United Automobile Workers Union, 42-44.

their resentment against the least scrupulous white merchants.[40] His testimony ran counter to the presumption that the rioting was meaningless, and, though confirmed by half a dozen witnesses, it, too, was disregarded by the commission.

Rejecting this and other evidence inconsistent with its preconceptions, the McCone Commission found three main reasons for the Los Angeles riots (other than police-Negro misunderstanding and irresponsible Negro leadership): excessive unemployment, inferior education, and inadequate transportation. The jobless Negro cannot attain a decent standard of living, the commission argued, nor can he assume responsibility for his family. Hence his self-esteem wanes, and his community ties erode; welfare, which feeds his children, intensifies his sense of dependency. Training the Negro worker to compete in the labor market is one solution. Also, the commission insisted, the Negro youngster cannot understand what is taught in the schools because he is culturally deprived. Nor can the schools help; they have insufficient equipment and a limited curriculum, too few experienced teachers and too many double sessions. To educate the Negro student so that he can be trained for skilled employment is another solution. Furthermore, the commission contended, the Negro is sorely inconvenienced as a worker and a student because the ghetto is isolated from Los Angeles. And it is isolated because in a metropolis which lacks adequate mass transit facilities only fourteen per cent of the families in southcentral Los Angeles, as opposed to over fifty per cent in Los Angeles County, own automobiles. Improving transportation in Los Angeles, and thereby facilitating movement in and out of the ghetto, is yet another solution.[41]

The McCone Commission's recommendations are consistent with its preconceptions, too. To reduce unemployment, it proposed that government, business, and labor create a job training and placement center in southcentral Los Angeles, that federal and state authorities insure that due advantage is taken of the available training programs and job opportunities, and, less vital, that the California legislature require employers and unions to disclose the racial composition of their employes and members. To upgrade educa-

[40] Ibid., Testimony of Thomas Reddin, Los Angeles Police Department, 21.
[41] MCR, 38-47, 49-60, 65-67.

-130-

tion, it urged that a permanent pre-school program be established in the Negro ghetto to assist three-year olds to develop the skills required to learn to read and write, and that certain elementary and junior high schools there—designated "emergency schools"—be authorized to set up literacy programs with classes limited to twenty-two students and special services provided by supplementary personnel. To improve transportation, it recommended that all transit companies in greater Los Angeles be consolidated with the Southern California Rapid Transit District, and that public authority subsidize the District to expand service in the ghetto[42]—a recommendation partially implemented when the U.S. Department of Housing and Urban Development granted $2.7 million to the District in May 1966.[43]

Neither these recommendations nor the reasons underlying them are satisfactory, however. Unemployment in southcentral Los Angeles—which, by the U.S. Census Bureau's conservative estimate, exceeds ten per cent—is indeed excessive. But inadequate training is only one among many reasons for unemployment, and unemployment is only one among many economic problems in the ghetto.[44] About these reasons—job shortages, racial discrimination, and criminal records—and these problems—irregular employment and low-wage employment—the McCone Commission said almost nothing. Education in the Negro ghetto—where, according to commission consultant Kenneth A. Martyn, test scores in all subjects and at all grades are extremely low—is inferior, too. But approximately one Negro in four who graduates from high school in southcentral Los Angeles cannot find employment anyway, and many others must settle for menial jobs.[45] To urge Negroes to acquire an education under these circumstances, as the McCone Commission did, is unfair and perhaps even unsafe. Finally, it is undeniable that mass transit is woefully inadequate in southcentral

[42] Ibid., 47-48, 60-61, 67-68.
[43] New York Times, May 28, 1966.
[44] U.S. Department of Labor, "Sub-Employment in the Slums of Los Angeles" ([Washington, D.C.], 1966). For the commission's position on criminal records and employment opportunities, see MCR, 47.
[45] Kenneth A. Martyn, "Report on Education to the Governor's Commission on the Los Angeles Riots" (Nov. 1965), 2-30, MCA, XVIII; U.S. Department of Labor, The Negroes in the United States: Their Social and Economic Situation (Washington, D.C., 1966), 24-25.

Los Angeles as well as in greater Los Angeles. But, according to a 1965 census, fully sixty-five per cent of the families in the Negro ghetto, and not, as reported by the McCone Commission, only fourteen per cent, own one or more cars.[46] The southcentral ghetto is indeed isolated, but not for reasons as simple and reassuring as dreadful bus service.

The McCone Commission's explanations and recommendations are particularly incomplete with regard to consumer exploitation and racial discrimination. The commission admitted that many witnesses charged that white merchants systematically exploit colored consumers in southcentral Los Angeles. But it insisted that low-income consumers are at a disadvantage everywhere, not only in the Negro ghetto, and denied that there was a correlation between the charges of consumer exploitation and the patterns of looting and burning.[47] To relieve consumer exploitation it merely recommended establishment of educational programs and expansion of legal services in the Watts area.. The commission's findings were derived from a blatant distortion of the evidence,. however, and do not withstand careful scrutiny. Consumer exploitation is a function of race as well as poverty, of customers without credit, high-risk businesses, and merchants without scruples. The correlation between rioting, especially arson, and consumer exploitation is imperfect, but, the archives reveal, convincing just the same.[48] And the commission's recommendations are inadequate because, if implemented, they would not increase consumer credit, reduce business risks, or curtail mercantile cupidity in southcentral Los Angeles.

If the McCone Commission minimized consumer exploitation it ignored racial discrimination. For this the witnesses were not to blame. One after another—and sometimes with much eloquence—they spoke of discrimination. They testified that it started when

[46] U.S. Bureau of the Census, *Current Population Reports*, Series P-23, No. 17, "Special Census Survey of the South and East Los Angeles Areas: November 1965" (Washington, D.C., 1966), 13.
[47] MCR, 62-65.
[48] MCA, V, Testimony of Harvey Claybrook, an accountant formerly employed in Watts, 8-13; XII, Testimony of Thomas Reddin, Los Angeles Police Department, 21-22; XIII, Testimony of Helen Nelson, consumer counsel, state of California, 1-14. See, also, Rustin, 29-30; Cohen and Murphy, 111, 132; David Caplovitz, *The Poor Pay More: Consumer Practices of Low-Income Families* (New York, 1963), passim.

colored people first migrated to southern California at the turn of the century and still persists today, fully fifty years and half a million Negroes later. They also testified that most whites, not only patrolmen, politicians, realtors, and merchants, treat most Negroes as unworthy, undesirable, and, even more aggravating, inferior.[49] Yet their testimony, which, while subjective, was quite restrained, made no impact on the McCone Commission—and for good reason. The commission could not concede that Negro resentment of racial discrimination (as well as economic deprivation and consumer exploitation) was justified, or that assaults on white passers-by and looting and burning of neighborhood stores were manifestations of these grievances, without abandoning its preconceptions about the riots. For that reason the McCone Comission failed to discover the conditions underlying the riots in Los Angeles and to devise recommendations which might prevent future rioting there.

IV

The McCone Commission also failed to explain why the customary restraints on rioting were inoperative in the southcentral ghetto in August 1965. To be sure, it did devote a large amount of its limited time to investigate the ineffectiveness of external restraints—paramilitary and military power—in Los Angeles. It questioned Chief Parker, Lieutenant Governor Anderson, and Lieutenant General Roderic Hill, commander of the California National Guard about the coordination of local, state, and national police forces. It examined their activities during the riots to determine why the National Guard was not ordered in earlier—which it assumed, perhaps rightly, would have ended the rioting sooner.[50] To an observer who considers the Los Angeles riots a problem of Negro ghettos and not of police strategy, the questioning seems wide of the mark. The commission's finding, that Lieutenant Governor Anderson delayed unduly in responding to Chief Parker's request

[49] Loren Miller, "Relationship of Racial Residential Segregation to Los Angeles Riots" (Oct. 7, 1965), MCA, X; ibid., XIV, Testimony of Sue Welch, a junior high school teacher in Watts, 17-22, 47-48.
[50] Ibid., III, Testimony of Lieutenant Governor Glenn Anderson; VIII, Testimony of Lieutenant General Roderic L. Hill; XI, Testimony of Police Chief William H. Parker.

for the National Guard, appears beside the point. And so does its conclusion that local law enforcement agencies and the National Guard should prepare plans for a quicker commitment and better deployment of the troops in the event of future emergencies.[51]

Far more serious, the McCone Commission spent little or no time analyzing the ineffectiveness of internal restraints in the ghetto. Indeed, it was so concerned about the damage done by the riots that it was oblivious to the risks run by the rioters. To riot with the support of the police, as the Irish did in New York in 1900, is one thing; to riot in spite of the opposition of the police and the military, as the Negroes did in Los Angeles in 1965, is quite another.[52] To discount this difference on the grounds that the patrolmen were outnumbered at the initial disturbance, that at first they attempted merely to contain the rioting, and that afterwards they exercised commendable restraint is to beg the question. However safe the rioters were during the first few days, they were in extreme peril during the last few days. By then all available police personnel and over 15,000 guardsmen were assigned to southcentral Los Angeles with orders to fire when fired upon and to take whatever action necessary, short of indiscriminate slaughter, to quell the rioting.[53] Thus, for several days the Negro ghetto was a very dangerous place—so dangerous, in fact, that by the time the authorities pacified it 34 persons were dead, over 1,000 injured, and nearly 4,000 arrested, almost all of whom were colored.

Given the grave dangers to life, limb, and liberty at the peak and near the end of the riots, it is not surprising that a majority of ghetto residents sought the safety of their homes. What is surprising is that a large minority, totaling scores of thousands of people, congregated in the streets and participated in the rioting anyway. The McCone Commission implied that their action reflected the growing sense of desperation among the Negro riffraff. This implication is unacceptable, however, not only because it misconstrues the composition of the rioters and discounts the risks involved in the riots, but also because the history of other under-

[51] MCR, 17, 19.
[52] Citizens Protective League, Story of the Riot ([New York], 1900); Gilbert Osofsky, Harlem: The Making of a Ghetto, Negro New York 1890-1930 (New York, 1966), 46-52.
[53] MCR, 17-20; MCA, II, passim; Cohen and Murphy, Chaps. 15-21.

privileged groups in the United States—native Americans in Appalachia, Puerto Ricans in New York, and Mexicans in southern California—reveals that poverty and functional illiteracy do not necessarily lead to rioting.[54] It is unacceptable, too, because it simply does not explain why Los Angeles' Negroes, however intense their resentment, refused to abide by the time-honored strategy expressed in the aphorism "Cheese it, the cops!" why they, unlike other ethnic minorities before them, insisted instead on a direct confrontation with the authorities, and why, in sum, they disregarded the cardinal restraints on rioting in the United States.

There are several such restraints: fear of arrest, and possible conviction and imprisonment, which is inconvenient at the time and burdensome later on; concern for personal safety, the reluctance to chance life and limb, especially when the opposition is far stronger; and, perhaps most compelling, the presence of faith, or the absence of despair, the conviction that necessary changes can be secured through legitimate channels and that the point at which violence is the only recourse has not yet been reached.[55] Accordingly, the rioting of the Negroes in the face of grave dangers meant not only that the grievances provoking them were insupportable, but also that the restraints inhibiting them were inoperative. To claim that these circumstances were complementary and equally crucial prerequisites for the 1965 riots is not to deny that the grievances generated the resentment which weakened the restraints. Indeed, this is just what happened in southcentral Los Angeles. It is rather to insist that there are certain other conditions—completely overlooked by the McCone Commission—which have further undermined the internal restraints on rioting in the Negro ghetto. And if the reason these conditions were overlooked can be uncovered, the explanation for the commission's failure will be sharply clarified.

Why the restraints on rioting were inoperative can be quickly outlined. To begin with, fear of arrest did not restrain the rioters

[54] The McCone Commission lumped the Mexicans and Negroes in Los Angeles together just the same. See MCR, 5.

[55] What I am suggesting here is not that these are the only restraints on rioting or that they function in similar ways in all groups and classes, but rather that these are the restraints which are considered, not without reason, crucial in American society.

because the overwhelming majority of them—or of the men at any rate—had already been arrested, if not convicted and imprisoned. The exact proportion has not been calculated, but seventy-five per cent is a reasonable estimate; and whether it is a trifle too low or too high is not critical because most of the other twenty-five per cent presume that they, too, will be arrested sooner or later—if not for rioting then for something else.[56] Concern for personal safety did not restrain the rioters either because they had been hardened to the point of indifference by the relentless assaults on life and limb in the Negro ghetto. The rioting, tumultuous though it was, did not mark a fundamental discontinuity in their experience, nor pose an extraordinary threat to their security; thus they were not compelled to refrain from participating because of the dangers involved.[57] Lastly, confidence in orderly social change did not restrain the rioters because, whatever their objective circumstances, they were convinced that their trust was misplaced. Indeed, according to surveys conducted in the Negro ghetto shorty after the riots, a substantial majority of the residents still believed that violence was either necessary or, if not, probable just the same.[58]

The reasons for these conditions can be briefly summarized. The extreme incidence of arrest is due in large part to preventative patrolling in the ghetto, a police practice which, in the name of rigorous law enforcement, subjects the Negroes to intensive surveillance, unwarranted suspicion, and outright harassment. The high level of violence is a consequence of the Negroes' tendency to resort to illegitimate enterprises when legitimate channels to success are obstructed and to express through aggression against other Negroes the resentment which cannot be directed against white people. And the dwindling confidence in orderly change is a reflection of the disparity between the rapid rise in the Negroes' ex-

[56] For nationwide estimates—the only ones available—see President's Commission on Law Enforcement, *The Challenge of Crime*, 75, and R. Christensen, "Projected Percentages of U.S. Population with Criminal Arrest and Conviction Records" (Aug. 18, 1966), report prepared for the commission. See, also, Cohen and Murphy, 208.

[57] President's Commission on Law Enforcement, *The Challenge of Crime*, 62; Marvin E. Wolfgang, *Crime and Race Conceptions and Misconceptions* (New York, 1964), 38-44.

[58] *MCA*, II, 32; Cohen and Murphy, 207; John F. Kraft, Inc., "Attitudes of Negroes," 7.

pectations and the more gradual advance in their achievements, a disparity which is more pronounced in the nineteen-sixties than at any other time in the twentieth century.[59] However brief this summary, one conclusion does emerge: the conditions undermining the restraints and the reasons underlying the conditions are all manifestations of slum (as well as ghetto) life in southcentral Los Angeles. For it is only in the slums, though not only in Los Angeles slums and not only in Negro slums, that preventative patrolling is practiced so intensively, illegitimate enterprises operate so openly, and minority groups are frustrated so frequently in their quest for a better life.

To the McCone Commission, however, southcentral Los Angeles was not a slum—not an urban gem, it conceded, but not a slum either.[60] Hence there was no reason for the commission to probe for the conditions which weakened the restraints on rioting in the ghetto. Commissioner Warren M. Christopher's examination of Judge Loren Miller provides a good starting point for determining why the commission failed to probe for these conditions. Christopher remarked that he returned from a recent visit to other Negro ghettos surprisingly reassured. "I wouldn't say that this [Watts] is a garden spot of South Los Angeles," he said, "but I see street after street of small well-kept homes and I find the contrast between that and the large tenement structures in New York and Philadelphia ... quite striking."[61] What about this contrast, he asked? Miller, who was less impressed, answered that Watts did not resemble Harlem, but neither did Los Angeles resemble New York; and in any case the southcentral ghetto was a slum. Other witnesses agreed, insisting that closer observation of the Watts vicinity would have revealed that one of every three houses there was dilapidated or deteriorated. And so did others, who stressed that by any social, economic, or psychological—as opposed to

---

[59] Diane Fisher, "Police Investigatory Practices" (1966), report prepared for the President's Commission on Law Enforcement and Administration of Justice; Richard A. Cloward and Lloyd E. Ohlin, Deliquency and Opportunity (Glencoe, 1960), Chaps. 1, 2, 4; Abraham Kardiner and Lionel Ovesey, The Mark of Oppression (Cleveland, 1962), Chap. 5; William Brink and Louis Harris, The Negro Revolution in America (New York, 1964), Chaps. 1, 2; Fogelson, "The 1960's Riots," Chap. IV.

[60] MCR, 3.

[61] MCA, X, Testimony of Judge Loren Miller, 17-18.

physical—criteria, southcentral Los Angeles was unquestionably a slum.[62]

On what, then, if not the testimony of the witnesses, did the McCone Commission base its conclusion that southcentral Los Angeles was not a slum? The commission's observation that the streets were wide, clean, and lined with trees and that the houses were one- and two-family dwellings only repeats the question. For what the commission observed depended on what it deemed worth observing, which, in turn, depended on how it conceived of a slum. And despite a rash of studies showing that physical condition is only one, and by no means the principal, measure of a slum, the commission's conception was purely environmental.[63] By this conception, which the commission shares with most Americans, a slum is defined by its deviation from a middle-class residential suburb. And on the surface Watts does not deviate very much—a fact which no doubt helps explain why so many Los Angeles whites found the 1965 riots beyond belief. Indeed, this conception of a slum is altogether indifferent to the wide range of social, economic, and psychological indicators of community pathology. So, accordingly, was the McCone Commission, and for that reason it overlooked the extreme incidence of arrest, high level of violence, and dwindling confidence in orderly change which rendered the restraints on rioting inoperative in southcentral Los Angeles.

V

The McCone Commission also misinterpreted the Negro leaders' role in the Los Angeles riots. The leaders, the commission argued, incited the ghetto residents by various inflammatory activities. They denounced the disparities between the grandiose promises of the anti-poverty program and the patent inadequacy of its provisions and protracted bickering over its implementation. They also encouraged Los Angeles' Negroes to feel affronted by the pas-

[62] Ibid., III, Testimony of Herb Atkinson, vice-president, South Los Angeles Transportation Company, 25; X, Testimony of John C. Monning, superintendent, Los Angeles Department of Building and Safety, 5-8; XIII, Testimony of Winston Slaughter, Compton Junior College student, 5-29; XIV, Testimony of Edward Warren, Watts real estate broker, 9-11.

[63] MCR, 3, 75-80; MCA, X, Testimony of Judge Loren Miller, 17-18. See Herbert J. Gans, The Urban Villagers (Glencoe, 1962), Chaps. 1, 14.

sage of Proposition 14, a state-wide referendum which repealed California's fair housing act and precluded future fair housing legislation. (The commission's choice of words was perplexing here; given the obvious implications of Proposition 14, surely the Negroes needed no encouragement to feel affronted by its passage.) And inspired by reports of civil disobedience and outright violence elsewhere in the United States, they even exhorted Negroes to devise extreme and illegal remedies for wrongs in Los Angeles. On the basis of these findings, the McCone Commission recommended that Negro leaders curb their extremism and—in the phrase of one commissioner, the Negro pastor who disagreed with this recommendation—"put the lid on protest."[64]

These findings are not corroborated by the testimony offered at the hearings, however. The Negro leaders, the witnesses pointed out, had attempted to channel the ghetto's discontent into constructive outlets long before the riots.[65] They were, after all, middle-class in outlook, personally confident in orderly change, and professionally committed to non-violent protest. They also realized that rioting would not only endanger the rioters, but, by alienating their friends and comforting their enemies, undermine the civil rights movement as well. Once the riots erupted, moreover, the Negro leaders perceived that, their positions notwithstanding, they simply were not leading. They understood that the rioters were challenging their leadership in the Negro community and subverting their positions vis-à-vis white society. They could, and did, denounce the conditions responsible for the riots, but the intensity of the outbursts demanded something stronger than words. Hence, other than to join the rioting and assume its direction—which they were unwilling (and probably unable) to do—the Negro leaders had no alternative but to try to restrain the rioters. And from the beginning to very near the end of the riots, as the witnesses testified, these leaders roamed the stricken streets of Los Angeles doing precisely that.[66]

[64] *MCR*, 2, 85-88.
[65] *MCA*, IV, Testimony of Reverend H. Hartford Brookins, 24-32; Harry M. Scoble, "Negro Leadership Study: Tentative Findings" (1966), 9, unpublished paper written for the U.S. Office of Economic Opportunity.
[66] *MCA*, V, Testimony of Wendell Collins, first vice-chairman of CORE, 6-25; Dymally, "Statement"; Cohen and Murphy, 119-20.

364 | POLITICAL SCIENCE QUARTERLY

Yet none of them was successful.[67] In stressing that local leadership (not to mention national leadership) was incapable of restraining the rioters, I am not implying that the rioters were easily restrained; excitement was too great, grievances too strong, and customary restraints too weak. I am suggesting that the outbreak of rioting in southcentral Los Angeles revealed that Negro leaders had failed not simply to ameliorate the real hardships in the ghetto but also to direct the attendant resentment into non-violent channels. I am suggesting, too, that the timing of the riots—they started late each evening and stopped early each morning—provided Negro leaders with an opportunity to meet with residents of the ghetto under relatively calm circumstances every day, and yet they totally failed to exploit this opportunity. Taken together, these failures highlight the ineffectiveness of moderate leadership, individual and institutional, in southcentral Los Angeles, a problem much more serious than the McCone Commission's unfounded allegations about the extremism and irresponsibility of the Negro leaders.

There are several reasons why Negro leadership is ineffective in the southcentral ghetto. There is the intransigence of white Los Angeles, an attitude responsible for the approval of Proposition 14 and other discriminatory actions which have impaired the Negro leaders' prestige. There are the apathy of lower- and working-class Negroes, the competition of militant black nationalist organizations, and the absence of a distinctive Negro culture in the United States. There is also the weakness of Negro voluntary associations, which is largely due to the assumption of their traditional functions by public authority, private enterprise, and the mass media. And there is the lower- and working-class Negroes' antagonism to the middle-class Negroes who alone have the time, money, and energy to organize cohesive groups and fill positions of leadership.[68] These reasons cannot and need not be described in any depth here. One other reason is, however, worth discussing in more detail because it has implications for an examination of the

[67] *Ibid.*, 130-31. Neither were Negro leaders in other cities; see Federal Bureau of Investigation, "Report on the 1964 Riots" (Sept. 18, 1964), 3.

[68] *MCA*, III, Testimony of Herb Atkinson, 25; statement by Gloster B. Current in "Community Unrest: Causes, Effects, Prevention, Cure," transcript of NAACP seminar, Columbus, Ohio, April 2, 1966, pp. 27-28.

McCone Commission as well as for a consideration of Negro leadership. That reason is the pronounced indifference of middle-class Negroes to the problems of the inhabitants and institutions of southcentral Los Angeles.

This is not to imply that middle-class Negroes are unsympathetic to the plight of lower- and working-class Negroes in Los Angeles; with a few exceptions, they are not. It is rather to argue that they have not displayed the same concern for the southcentral ghetto that middle-class Italians and Jews in Boston and New York showed for the North End and Lower East Side.[69] Middle-class Negroes in Los Angeles have instead left the ghetto physically and/or spiritually. They have left it physically not only because social conditions there do not meet middle-class standards, but also because housing there is vastly inferior to housing elsewhere in Los Angeles. The U.S. Census of 1965 reveals that houses in southcentral Los Angeles are the most overcrowed, substandard, and overpriced in the metropolis.[70] Middle-class Negroes have also left the Los Angeles ghetto spiritually to dissociate themselves not only from lower- and working-class people, a common practice of middle-class Americans whatever their color, but from what is for them, as the plantation was for their fathers, the embodiment of the Negroes' ignominious position in American society, the symbol of their subordination and segregation.[71] Within or without the southcentral ghetto, the middle-class Negroes are not of it, and thus cannot lead it.

What underlies the physical and/or spiritual flight of middle-class Negroes from the southcentral ghetto is the widespread system of involuntary residential segregation in greater Los Angeles. Just how widespread the system is has been too well documented elsewhere to warrant further proof here,[72] but its involuntary char-

[69] Gans, 298; Arthur Aryeh Goren, "The New York Kehillah: 1908-1922" (Columbia University Doctoral Dissertation, 1966), passim; Moses Rischin, The Promised City (Cambridge, 1962), Chap. 6.
[70] U.S. Bureau of the Census, "Characteristics of the South and East Los Angeles Areas," 34-37. See, also, Fred E. Case, "Housing in the Los Angeles Riot Area," MCA, XVII.
[71] MCA, III, Testimony of Herb Atkinson, 25. For the nationwide pattern, see E. Franklin Frazier, Black Bourgeoisie (Chicago, 1957), Part II; Louis E. Lomax, The Negro Revolt (New York, 1962), 202.
[72] Karl E. Taeuber and Alma F. Taeuber, Negroes in Cities (Chicago, 1965), passim.

acter is worth stressing. Negroes, unlike Mexicans and other new-comers, did not choose to live as a group in Los Angeles; far from having chosen at all, they were simply compelled to reside to-gether.[73] And the consequences were as unfortunate as they were inevitable. So long as Negroes were denied access to metropolitan Los Angeles' real estate market and so long as they were deprived of the chance to move freely if dissatisfied with the quality or cost of their housing, they were confined to overcrowded, substandard, and overpriced dwellings. Also, so long as they lived in southcen-tral Los Angeles only because there were no alternatives and so long as they regarded it as a place of confinement, they perceived the ghetto as the emblem of their subordination, segregation, and inferiority. Under these circumstances middle-class Negroes fled the ghetto in one way or another whenever by dint of herculean effort they could do so.

Yet the McCone Commission did nothing more than admit that involuntary residential segregation is practiced in metropolitan Los Angeles.[74] It did not consider its consequences or recommend its elimination, nor did it point out the implications of Proposition 14. For this the witnesses were once again free of fault. One after another they explained how involuntary residential segregation is implemented in Los Angeles and how the Negro community is victimized by this practice. Yet the McCone Commission ignored them because their testimony revealed the tremendous stakes that Los Angeles whites have in perpetuating the Negro ghetto. Mer-chants who overcharge customers, manufacturers who underpay laborers, and landlords who exploit tenants are only the most obvi-ous beneficiaries. Less evident but more numerous are the home-owners who spend their lives in all-white suburbs and the parents who send their children to all-white schools. For the McCone Com-mission to have investigated involuntary residential segregation would have obliged it to abandon its preconceptions that the Los

[73] Miller, 1-9; Robert M. Fogelson, The Fragmented Metropolis: Los Angeles, 1850-1930 (to be published in Cambridge, Mass., 1967), Chap. 9. See, also, Charles Abrams, Forbidden Neighbors (New York, 1955), Chaps. XII-XIV, XVI-XVIII; [California] Commission on Race and Housing, Where Shall We Live (Berkeley and Los Angeles, 1958), 36.
[74] MCR, 75-80.

Angeles riots were manifestations of economic, not racial, problems and individual, not social, deficiencies.

Here as elsewhere, then, the McCone Commission offered inadequate recommendations based on erroneous analyses derived from untenable assumptions. And in so doing it demeaned the rioters, belittled their grievances, misunderstood their ghetto, misconstrued the riots, and thereby discouraged efforts to devise imperative and more radical reforms. As the official version of the Los Angeles riots, moreover, "Violence in the City" has shaped public policy—witness the federal subsidy to the Transit District—and also guided popular opinion. From it the residents of Los Angeles have either taken the conclusion that the rioting was meaningless or drawn the implication that the Negroes somehow lack the qualifications for responsible citizenship. That the McCone Commission provided them no other alternatives was not the least of its disservices to their community. Worse still, the commission reflected middle-class, white American ideas and values so well that its findings and recommendations, or facsimiles thereof, have also appeared in many official observations about other recent riots[75] —and, not surprisingly, with no more validity. Not until white America abandons the preconceptions about rioting, law enforcement, slums, and ghettos which misled the McCone Commission will it recognize the riots of the nineteen-sixties for what they were—articulate protests against genuine grievances in the Negro ghettos.

[75] See P. W. Homer, City Manager, "Report to the Rochester City Council on the Riots of July 1964" (April 27, 1965); New York *Times*, July 22, Aug. 4, 1964.

THE WATTS "MANIFESTO"

AND THE McCONE REPORT

THE WATTS "MANIFESTO"

& THE McCONE REPORT

BAYARD RUSTIN

THE RIOTS IN the Watts section of Los
Angeles last August continued for six
days, during which 34 persons were killed, 1,032
were injured, and some 3,952 were arrested.
Viewed by many of the rioters themselves as their
"manifesto," the uprising of the Watts Negroes
brought out in the open, as no other aspect of
the Negro protest has done, the despair and hatred
that continue to brew in the Northern ghettoes
despite the civil-rights legislation of recent years
and the advent of "the war on poverty." With
national attention focused on Los Angeles, Governor Edward P. Brown created a commission of
prominent local citizens, headed by John A.
McCone, to investigate the causes of the riots and
to prescribe remedies against any such outbreaks
in the future. Just as the violent confrontation on
the burning streets of Watts told us much about
the underlying realities of race and class relations
in America—summed up best, perhaps, by the
words of Los Angeles Police Chief William
Parker, "We're on top and they're on the bottom"

—so does the McCone Report, published under the title *Violence in the City—An End or a Beginning?*, tell us much about the response of our political and economic institutions to the Watts "manifesto."

Like the much-discussed Moynihan Report, the McCone Report is a bold departure from the standard government paper on social problems. It goes beyond the mere recital of statistics to discuss, somewhat sympathetically, the real problems of the Watts community—problems like unemployment, inadequate schools, dilapidated housing—and it seems at first glance to be leading toward constructive programs. It never reaches them, however, for, again like the Moynihan Report, it is ambivalent about the basic reforms that are needed to solve these problems and therefore shies away from spelling them out too explicitly. Thus, while it calls for the creation of 50,000 new jobs to compensate for the "spiral of failure" that it finds among the Watts Negroes, the McCone Report does not tell us how these jobs are to be created or obtained and instead recommends existing programs which have already shown themselves to be inadequate. The Moynihan Report, similarly, by emphasizing the breakdown of the Negro family, also steers clear of confronting the thorny issues of Negro unemployment as such.

By appearing to provide new viewpoints and fresh initiatives while at the same time repeating, if in more sophisticated and compassionate terms, the standard white stereotypes and shibboleths about Negroes, the two reports have become controversial on both sides of the Negro question. On the one hand, civil-rights leaders can point to the recognition in these reports of the need for jobs and training, and for other economic and social programs to aid the Negro family, while conservatives can find confirmed in their pages the Negro penchant for violence, the excessive agitation against law and order by the civil-rights movement, or the high rates of crime and illegitimacy in the Negro community; on the other hand, both sides have criticized the reports for feeding ammunition to the opposition. Unfortunately, but inevitably, the emphasis on *Negro* behavior in both reports has stirred up an abstract debate over the interpretation of data rather than suggesting programs for dealing with the existing and very concrete situation in which American Negroes find themselves. For example, neither report is concerned about segregation and both tacitly assume that the Civil Rights Acts of 1964 and 1965 are already destroying this system. In the case of the McCone Report, this leaves the writers free to discuss the problems of Negro housing, education, and unemployment in great detail without attacking the conditions of de facto segregation that underly them.

THE ERRORS and misconceptions of the McCone Report are particularly revealing because it purports to deal with the realities of the Watts riots rather than with the abstractions of the Negro family. The first distortion of these realities occurs in the opening chapter—"The Crisis: An Overview"—where, after briefly discussing the looting and beatings, the writers conclude that "The rioters seem to have been caught up in an insensate rage of destruction." Such an image may reflect the fear of the white community that Watts had run amok during six days in August, but it does not accurately describe the major motive and mood of the riots, as subsequent data in the report itself indicate. While it is true that Negroes in the past have often turned the violence inflicted on them by society in upon themselves—"insensate rage" would perhaps have been an appropriate phrase for the third day of the 1964 Harlem riots— the whole point of the outbreak in Watts was that it marked the first major rebellion of Negroes against their own masochism and was carried on with the express purpose of asserting that they would no longer quietly submit to the deprivation of slum life.

This message came home to me over and over again when I talked with the young people in Watts during and after the riots, as it will have come home to those who watched the various television documentaries in which the Negroes of the community were permitted to speak for themselves. At a street-corner meeting in Watts when the riots were over, an unemployed youth of about twenty said to me, "We won." I asked him: "How have you won? Homes have been destroyed, Negroes are lying dead in the streets, the stores from which you buy food and clothes are destroyed, and people are bringing you relief." His reply was significant: "We won because we made the whole world pay attention to us. The police chief never came here before; the mayor always stayed uptown. We made them come." Clearly it was no accident that the riots proceeded along an almost direct path to City Hall.

Nor was the violence along the way random and "insensate." Wherever a store-owner identified himself as a "poor working Negro trying to make a business" or as a "Blood Brother," the mob passed the store by. It even spared a few white businesses that allowed credit or time purchases, and it made a point of looting and destroying stores that were notorious for their high prices and hostile manners. The McCone Report itself observes that "the rioters concentrated on food markets, liquor stores, clothing stores, department stores, and pawn shops." The authors "note with interest that no residences were deliberately burned, that damage to schools, libraries, public buildings was minimal and that certain types of business establishments, notably service stations and automobile dealers, were for the most part unharmed." It is also worth noting that the rioters were much more inclined to destroy the stock of the liquor stores they broke into than to steal it, and that according to the McCone Report, "there is no evidence that the rioters made any attempt to steal narcotics from pharmacies . . . which were looted and burned."

This is hardly a description of a Negro community that has run amok. The largest number of arrests were for looting—not for arson or shooting. Most of the people involved were not habitual thieves; they were members of a deprived group who seized a chance to possess things that all the dinning affluence of Los Angeles had never given them. There were innumerable touching examples of this behavior. One married couple in their sixties was seen carrying a couch to their home, and when its weight became too much for them, they sat down and rested on it until they could pick it up again. Langston Hughes tells of another woman who was dragging a sofa .through the streets and who stopped at each intersection and waited for the traffic light to turn green. A third woman went out with her children to get a kitchen set, and after bringing it home, she discovered they needed one more chair in order to feed the whole family together; they went back to get the chair and all of them were arrested.

I F THE McCone Report misses the point of the Watts riots, it shows even less understanding of their causes. To place these in perspective, the authors begin by reviewing the various outbursts in the Negro ghettoes since the summer of 1964 and quickly come up with the following explanations: "Not enough jobs to go around, and within this scarcity not enough by a wide margin of a character which the untrained Negro could fill.... Not enough schooling to meet the special needs of the disadvantaged Negro child whose environment from infancy onward places him under a serious handicap." Finally, "a resentment, even hatred, of the police as a symbol of authority."

For the members of the special commission these are the fundamental causes of the current Negro plight and protest, which are glibly summed up in the ensuing paragraph by the statement that "Many Negroes moved to the city in the last generation and are totally unprepared to meet the conditions of city life." I shall be discussing these "causes" in detail as we go along, but it should be noted here that the burden of responsibility has already been placed on these hapless migrants to the cities. There is not one word about the conditions, economic as well as social, that have pushed Negroes out of the rural areas; nor is there one word about whether the cities have been willing and able to meet the demand for jobs, adequate housing, proper schools. After all, one could as well say that it is the *cities* which have been "totally unprepared" to meet the "conditions of *Negro* life," but the moralistic bias of the McCone Report, involving as it does an emphasis on the decisions of men rather than the pressure of social forces, continually operates in the other direction.

The same failure of awareness is evident in the report's description of the Los Angeles situation (the Negro areas of Los Angeles "are not urban gems, neither are they slums," the Negro population "has exploded," etc.). The authors do concede that the Los Angeles transportation system is the "least adequate of any major city," but even here they fail to draw the full consequences of their findings. Good, cheap transportation is essential to a segregated working-class population in a big city. In Los Angeles a domestic worker, for example, must spend about $1.50 and 1½ to 2 hours to get to a job that pays $6 or $7 a day. This both discourages efforts to find work and exacerbates the feeling of isolation.

A neighborhood such as Watts may seem beautiful when compared to much of Harlem (which, in turn, is an improvement over the Negro section of Mobile, Alabama)—but it is still a ghetto. The housing is run-down, public services are inferior, the listless penned-in atmosphere of segregation is oppressive. Absentee landlords are the rule, and most of the businesses are owned by whites: neglect and exploitation reign by day, and at night, as one Watts Negro tersely put it, "There's just the cops and us."

The McCone Report, significantly, also ignores the political atmosphere of Los Angeles. It refers, for example, to the repeal in 1964 of the Rumford Act—the California fair-housing law—in these words: "In addition, many Negroes here felt and were encouraged to feel that they had been affronted by the passage of Proposition 14." Affronted, indeed! The largest state in the Union, by a three-to-one majority, abolishes one of its own laws against discrimination and Negroes are described as regarding this as they might the failure of a friend to keep an engagement. What they did feel—and without any need of encouragement—

was that while the rest of the North was passing civil-rights laws and improving opportunities for Negroes, their own state and city were rushing to reinforce the barriers against them.

The McCone Report goes on to mention two other "aggravating events in the twelve months prior to the riot." One was the failure of the poverty program to "live up to [its] press notices," combined with reports of "controversy and bickering" in Los Angeles over administering the program. The second "aggravating event" is summed up by the report in these words:

> Throughout the nation unpunished violence and disobedience to law were widely reported, and almost daily there were exhortations here and elsewhere, to take the most extreme and illegal remedies to right a wide variety of wrongs, real and supposed.

It would be hard to frame a more insidiously equivocal statement of the Negro grievance concerning law enforcement during a period that included the release of the suspects in the murder of the three civil-rights workers in Mississippi, the failure to obtain convictions against the suspected murderers of Medgar Evers and Mrs. Violet Liuzzo, the Gilligan incident in New York, the murder of Reverend James Reeb, and the police violence in Selma, Alabama—to mention only a few of the more notorious cases. And surely it would have been more to the point to mention that throughout the nation Negro demonstrations have almost invariably been non-violent, and that the major influence on the Negro community of the civil-rights movement has been the strategy of discipline and dignity. Obsessed by the few prophets of violent resistance, the McCone Commission ignores the fact that never before has an American group sent so many people to jail or been so severely punished for trying to uphold the law of the land.

IT IS NOT stretching things too far to find a connection between these matters and the treatment of the controversy concerning the role of the Los Angeles police. The report goes into this question at great length, finally giving no credence to the charge that the police may have contributed to the spread of the riots through the use of excessive force. Yet this conclusion is arrived at not from the point of view of the Watts Negroes, but from that of the city officials and the police. Thus, the report informs us, in judicial hearings that were held on 32 of the 35 deaths which occurred, 26 were ruled justifiable homicides, but the report —which includes such details as the precise time Mayor Yorty called Police Chief Parker and when exactly the National Guard was summoned—never tells us what a "justifiable homicide" is considered to be. It tells us that "of the 35 killed, one was a fireman, one was a deputy sheriff, and one was a Long Beach policeman," but it does not tell us how many Negroes were killed or injured by police or National Guardsmen. (Harry Fleischman of the American Jewish Committee reports that the fireman was killed by a falling wall; the deputy sheriff, by another sheriff's bullet; and the policeman, by another policeman's bullet.) We learn that of the 1,032 people reported injured, 90 were police· officers, 36 were firemen, 10 were National Guardsman, 23 were from government agencies. To find out that about 85 per cent of the injured were Negroes, we have to do our own arithmetic. The report contains no information as to how many of these were victims of police force, but one can surmise from the general pattern of the riots that few could have been victims of Negro violence.

The report gives credence to Chief Parker's assertion that the rioters were the "criminal element in Watts" yet informs us that of the 3,438 adults arrested, 1,164 had only minor criminal records and 1,232 had never been arrested before. Moreover, such statistics are always misleading. Most Negroes, at one time or another, have been picked up and placed in jail. I myself have been arrested twice in Harlem on charges that had no basis in fact: once for trying to stop a police officer from arresting the wrong man; the second time for asking an officer who was throwing several young men into a paddy wagon what they had done. Both times I was charged with interfering with an arrest and kept overnight in jail until the judge recognized me and dismissed the charges. Most Negroes are not fortunate enough to be recognized by judges.

Having accepted Chief Parker's view of the riots, the report goes on to absolve him of the charge of discrimination: "Chief Parker's statements to us and collateral evidence, such as his fairness to Negro officers, are inconsistent with his having such an attitude ['deep hatred of Negroes']. Despite the depth of feeling against Chief Parker expressed to us by so many witnesses, he is recognized even by many of his vocal critics as a capable Chief who directs an efficient police force and serves well this entire community."

I am not going to stress the usual argument that the police habitually mistreat Negroes. Every Negro knows this. There is scarcely any black man, woman, or child in the land who at some point or other has not been mistreated by a policeman. (A young man in Watts said, "The riots will continue because I, as a Negro, am immediately considered to be a criminal by the police and, if I have a pretty woman with me, she is a tramp even if she is my wife or mother.") Police Chief Parker, however, goes beyond the usual bounds. He does not recognize that he is prejudiced, and being both naïve and zealous about law and order, he is given to a dangerous fanaticism. His reference to the Negro rioters as "monkeys," and his "top . . . and bottom" description of the riots, speak for themselves, and they could only have further enraged and encouraged the rioters. His insistence on dealing with the outbreak in Watts as though it were the random work of a "criminal element" threatened to lead the community, as Martin Luther King remarked after the meeting he and I had with Chief Parker, "into potential holocaust." Though Dr. King and I have had considerable experience in talking with public officials who do not understand the Negro community, our discussions with Chief Parker and Mayor Samuel Yorty left us completely nonplussed. They both denied, for example, that there was any prejudice in Los

Angeles. When we pointed to the very heavy vote in the city for Proposition 14, they replied, "That's no indication of prejudice. That's personal choice." When I asked Chief Parker about his choice of language, he implied that this was the only language Negroes understood.

The impression of "blind intransigence and ignorance of the social forces involved" which Dr. King carried away from our meeting with Chief Parker is borne out by other indications. The cast of his political beliefs, for example, was evidenced during his appearance last May on the Manion Forum, one of the leading platforms of the radical right, in which (according to newspaper reports) he offered his "considered opinion that America today is in reality more than half pagan" and that "we have moved our form of government to a socialist form of government." Such opinions have a good deal of currency today within the Los Angeles police department. About a month before the riots, a leaflet describing Dr. King as a liar and a Communist was posted on the bulletin board of a Los Angeles police station, and only after the concerted efforts of various Negro organizations was this scurrilous pamphlet removed.

CERTAINLY these were "aggravating factors" that the McCone Report should properly have mentioned. But what is more important to understand is that even if every policeman in every black ghetto behaved like an angel and were trained in the most progressive of police academies, the conflict would still exist. This is so because the ghetto is a place where Negroes do not want to be and are fighting to get out of. When someone with a billy club and a gun tells you to behave yourself amid these terrible circumstances, he becomes a zoo keeper, demanding of you, as one of "these monkeys" (to use Chief Parker's phrase), that you accept abhorrent conditions. He is brutalizing you by insisting that you tolerate what you cannot, and ought not, tolerate.

In its blithe ignorance of such feelings, the McCone Report offers as one of its principal suggestions that speakers be sent to Negro schools to teach the students that the police are their friends and that their interests are best served by respect for law and order. Such public-relations gimmicks, of course, are futile—it is hardly a lack of contact with the police that creates the problem. Nor, as I have suggested, is it only a matter of prejudice. The fact is that when Negroes are deprived of work, they resort to selling numbers, women, or dope to earn a living; they must gamble and work in poolrooms. And when the policeman upholds the law, he is depriving them of their livelihood. A clever criminal in the Negro ghettoes is not unlike a clever "operator" in the white business world, and so long as Negroes are denied legitimate opportunities, no exhortations to obey the rules of the society and to regard the police as friends will have any effect.

This is not to say that relations between the police and the Negroes of Watts could not be improved. Mayor Yorty and Police Chief Parker might have headed off a full-scale riot had they refrained from denouncing the Negro leaders and agreed to meet with them early on. Over and over again—to repeat the point with which we began—the rioters claimed that violence was the only way they could get these officials to listen to them. The McCone Commission, however, rejects the proposal for an independent police review board and instead recommends that the post of Inspector General be established—under the authority of the Chief of Police—to handle grievances.

THE CONDITIONS of Negro life in Watts are not, of course, ignored by the McCone Report. Their basic structure is outlined in a section entitled "Dull, Devastating Spiral of Failure." Here we find that the Negro's "homelife destroys incentive"; that he lacks "experience with words and ideas"; that he is "unready and unprepared" in school; and that, "unprepared and unready," he "*slips* into the ranks of the unemployed" (my italics).

I would say, *is shoved*. It is time that we began to understand this "dull, devastating spiral of failure" and that we stopped attributing it to this or that characteristic of Negro life. In 1940, Edward

Wight Bakke described the effects of unemployment on family structure in terms of the following model: The jobless man no longer provides, credit runs out, the woman is forced to take a job; if relief then becomes necessary, the woman is regarded even more as the center of the family; the man is dependent on her, the children are bewildered, and the stability of the family is threatened and often shattered. Bakke's research dealt strictly with white families. The fact that Negro social scientists like E. Franklin Frazier and Kenneth Clark have shown that this pattern is typical among the Negro poor does not mean, then, that it stems from some inherent Negro trait or is the ineluctable product of Negro social history. If Negroes suffer more than others from the problems of family instability today, it is not because they are Negro but because they are so disproportionately unemployed, underemployed, and ill-paid.

Anyone looking for historical patterns would do well to consider the labor market for Negroes since the Emancipation. He will find that Negro men have consistently been denied the opportunity to enter the labor force in anything like proportionate numbers, have been concentrated in the unskilled and marginal labor and service occupations, and have generally required wartime emergencies to make any advances in employment, job quality, and security. Such advances are then largely wiped out when the economy slumps again.

In 1948, for example, the rates of Negro and white unemployment were roughly equal. During the next decade, however, Negro unemployment was consistently double that of whites, and among Negro teenagers it remained at the disastrously high figure which prevailed for the entire population during the Depression. It is true that the nation's improved economic performance in recent years has reduced the percentage of jobless Negroes from 12.6 per cent, which it reached in 1958 (12.5 per cent in 1961) to roughly 8.1 per cent today. Despite this progress, the rate of Negro unemployment continues to be twice as high as white (8.1 per cent as against 4.2 per cent). In other words, job discrimination remains constant. These statistics, moreover, conceal the persistence of Negro youth unemployment: in 1961, 24.7 per cent of those Negro teenagers not in school were out of work and it is estimated that in 1966 this incredible rate will only decline to 23.2 per cent. What this figure tells us is that the rise in Negro employment has largely resulted from the calling of men with previous experience back to work. This is an ominous trend, for it is estimated that in the coming year, 20 per cent of the new entrants into the labor force will be Negro (almost twice as high as the Negro percentage of the population). Approximately half of these young Negroes will not have the equivalent of a high-school education and they will be competing in an economy in which the demand for skill and training is increasing sharply.

Thus there is bound to be a further deterioration of the Negro's economic—and hence social—position, despite the important political victories being achieved by the civil-rights movement. For many young Negroes, who are learning that economic servitude can be as effective an instrument of discrimination as racist laws, the new "freedom" has already become a bitter thing indeed. No wonder that the men of Watts were incensed by reports that the poverty program was being obstructed in Los Angeles by administrative wrangling. (As I write this, the New York *Times* reports that political rivalries and ambitions have now virtually paralyzed the program in that area.)

How DOES THE McCone Report propose to halt this "dull, devastating spiral of failure"? First, through education—"our fundamental resource." The commission's analysis begins with a comparison of class size in white and Negro areas (the latter are referred to throughout as "disadvantaged areas" and Negro schools, as "disadvantaged schools"). It immediately notes that classes in the disadvantaged schools are slightly smaller; on the other hand, the more experienced teachers are likely to be found in the *non*-disadvantaged areas, and there is tremendous overcrowding in the disadvantaged schools because of double sessions. The buildings in the "disadvantaged areas are in better repair"; on the other hand, there are "cafeterias in the advantaged schools" but not in the disadvantaged schools, which also have no libraries. This random balance sheet of "resources" shows no sense of priorities; moreover, despite the alarming deficiencies it uncovers in the "disadvantaged schools," the McCone Report, in consistent fashion, places its emphasis on the Negro child's "deficiency in environmental experiences" and on "his homelife [which] all too often fails to give him incentive. . . ."

The two major recommendations of the commission in this area will hardly serve to correct the imbalances revealed. The first is that elementary and junior high schools in the "disadvantaged areas" which have achievement levels substantially below the city average should be designated "Emergency Schools." In each of these schools an emergency literacy program is to be established with a maximum of 22 students in each class and an enlarged and supportive corps of teachers. The second recommendation is to establish a permanent pre-school program to help prepare three- and four-year-old children to read and write.

W. T. Bassett, executive secretary of the Los Angeles AFL-CIO, has criticized the report for its failure to deal with education and training for adolescents and adults who are no longer in school. Another glaring omission is of a specific plan to decrease school segregation. While most of us now agree that the major goal of American education must be that of quality integrated schools, we cannot, as even the report suggests, achieve the quality without at the same time moving toward integration. The stated goal of the McCone Commission, however, is to "reverse the trend of de facto segregation" by improving the quality of the Negro schools: in short, separate but equal schools that do not disturb the existing social patterns which isolate the Negro child in his "disadvantaged areas."

That the commission's explicit concern for Negro problems falls short of its implicit concern for the status quo is also evident in its proposals for housing. It calls for the liberalization of credit and FHA-insured loans in "disadvantaged areas," the implementation of rehabilitation measures and other urban-renewal programs and, as its particular innovation, the creation of a "wide area data bank." Meanwhile it refuses to discuss, much less to criticize, the effect of Proposition 14 or to recommend a new fair-housing code. To protect the Negro against discrimination, the McCone Report supports the creation of a Commission on Human Relations, but does not present any proposals that would enable it to do more than collect information and conduct public-relations campaigns.

THE MOST crucial section of the report is the one on employment and, not unexpectedly, it is also the most ignorant, unimaginative, and conservative—despite its dramatic recommendation that 50,000 new jobs be created. On the matter of youth unemployment, the report suggests that the existing federal projects initiate a series of "attitudinal training" programs to help young Negroes develop the necessary motivation to hold on to these new jobs which are to come from somewhere that the commission keeps secret. This is just another example of the commission's continued reliance on public relations, and of its preoccupation with the "dull, devastating spiral" of Negro failure. The truth of the matter is that Negro youths cannot change their attitudes until they see that they can get jobs. When what they see is unemployment and their Economic Opportunity programs being manipulated in behalf of politicians, their attitudes will remain realistically cynical.

Once again, let me try to cut through the obscurantism which has increasingly come to cloud this issue of Negro attitudes. I am on a committee which administers the Apprenticeship Training Program of the Workers Defense League. For many years the League had heard that there were not enough Negro applicants to fill the various openings for apprenticeship training and had also repeatedly been told by vocational-school counselors that Negro students could not pay attention to key subjects such as English and mathematics. The League began its own recruitment and placement program two years ago and now has more than 500 apprentice applicants on file. When, last fall, Local 28 of the Sheetmetal Workers Union—to take one example—announced that a new admission test for apprentices was to be given soon, the League contacted those applicants who had indicated an interest in sheetmetal work. The young men came to the office, filled out a 10-page application form, filed a ten-dollar fee, and returned it to the Local 28 office. Then, five nights a week for three weeks, they came to Harlem, in many cases from Brooklyn and Queens, to be tutored. Most of the young men showed up for all fifteen sessions, and scored well on the test. At their interviews they were poised and confident. Eleven of these men finally were admitted to a class of 33. The WDL doesn't attribute this success to a miraculous program; it merely knows that when young people are told that at the end of a given period of study those who perform well will obtain decent work, then their attitudes will be markedly different from those who are sent off to a work camp with vague promises.

To cut the cost of job training programs, the McCone Commission avers that compensation "should not be necessary for those trainees who are receiving welfare support." Earlier in the report the authors point out that welfare services tend to destroy family life by giving more money to a woman who lives alone; yet they have the audacity to ask that the practice of not allowing men who are on family relief to earn an additional income be maintained for young men who are working and being trained. How is a young man to be adequately motivated if he cannot feel that his work is meaningful and necessary? The McCone Report would have us say to him, "There, there, young man, we're going to keep you off the streets —just putter around doing this make-work." But the young man knows that he can collect welfare checks and also hustle on street corners to increase his earnings. A man's share of a welfare allotment is pitifully small, but more than that, he should be paid for his work; and if one is interested in his morale, he should not be treated as a charity case.

Continuing with the problem of employment, the report recommends that "there should immediately be developed in the affected area a job training and placement center through the combined efforts of Negroes, employers, labor unions and government." In the absence of actual jobs, this would mean merely setting up a new division, albeit voluntary, of the unemployment insurance program. "Federal and state governments should seek to insure through development of new facilities and additional means of communication that advantage is taken of government and private training programs and employment opportunities in our disadvantaged communities." Perhaps the only thing the Job Corps program doesn't lack is publicity: last summer it received ten times as many applications as it could handle. Nor can new types of information centers and questionnaires provide 50,000 new jobs. They may provide positions for social workers and vocational counselors, but very few of them will be unemployed Negroes.

The report goes on: "Legislation should be enacted requiring employers with more than 250 employees and all labor unions to report annually to the state Fair Employment Practices Commission, the racial composition of the work force and membership." But an FEP Commission that merely collects information and propaganda is powerless. And even with the fullest cooperation of labor and management to promote equality of opportunity, the fact remains that there are not enough jobs in the Los Angeles area to go around, even for those who are fortunate enough to be included in the retraining programs. As long as unions cannot find work for many of their own members, there is not much they can do to help unemployed Negroes. And the McCone Report places much of its hope in private enterprise, whose response so far has been meager. The highest estimate of the number of jobs given to Los Angeles Negroes since the Watts crisis is less than 1,000.

THE NEGRO slums today are ghettoes of despair. In Watts, as elsewhere, there are the unemployable poor: the children, the aging, the permanently handicapped. No measure of employment or of economic growth will put an end to their misery, and only government programs can provide them with a decent way of life. The care of these people could be made a major area of job growth. Los Angeles officials could immediately train and put to work women and unemployed youths as school attendants, recreation counselors, practical nurses, and community workers. The federal government and the state of California could aid the people of Watts by beginning a massive public-works program to build needed housing, schools, hospitals, neighborhood centers, and transportation facilities: this, too, would create new jobs. In short, they could begin to develop the $100-billion freedom budget advocated by A. Philip Randolph.

Such proposals may seem impractical and even incredible. But what is truly impractical and incredible is that America, with its enormous wealth, has allowed Watts to become what it is and that a commission empowered to study this explosive situation should come up with answers that boil down to voluntary actions by business and labor, new public-relations campaigns for municipal agencies, and information-gathering for housing, fair-employment, and welfare departments. The Watts manifesto is a response to realities that the McCone Report is barely beginning to grasp. Like the liberal consensus which it embodies and reflects, the commission's imagination and political intelligence appear paralyzed by the hard facts of Negro deprivation it has unearthed, and it lacks the political will to demand that the vast resources of contemporary America be used to build a genuinely great society that will finally put an end to these deprivations. And what is most impractical and incredible of all is that we may very well continue to teach impoverished, segregated, and ignored Negroes that the only way they can get the ear of America is to rise up in violence.

WHITEWASH OVER WATTS:

THE FAILURE OF THE

McCONE COMMISSION REPORT

Whitewash Over Watts

The failure of the McCone Commission report

ROBERT BLAUNER

On August 24, 1965, just one week after public order had been restored in the south-central area of Los Angeles known as Watts, Governor Pat Brown of California announced the appointment of an eight-man commission of leading citizens. In his charge to the group (which came to be known as the McCone Commission, after its Chairman, John A. McCone, former head of the CIA), Brown asked it to "prepare an accurate chronology and description of the riots"; to "probe deeply the immediate and underlying causes of the riots"; and finally to "develop recommendations for action designed to prevent a recurrence of these tragic disorders."

For what appears to have been political considerations connected with possible repercussions of the Watts affair on the 1966 gubernatorial campaign, the Commission was given December 1, 1965, as the deadline for the completion of its report. Thus only 100 days were available for a "deep and probing" analysis of the most destructive incidents of racial violence in American history.

In an atmosphere of speed-up that made work on an automobile assembly-line appear leisurely by comparison, the Commission held a series of sixty formal hearings before which eighty sworn witnesses, including city and police officials, leaders and citizens of the white and Negro communities, eventually appeared. It also selected a full-time staff of thirty, primarily lawyers and legal-oriented investigators, to carry out the day-to-day work of assembling data and preparing to write the report. The staff called upon the services of twenty-six consultants (chiefly university professors in the social sciences) for advice and the sub-contracting of research; interviewed ninety persons from the 4,000 arrested; and opened an office in the riot area to receive testimony from Negro citizens. After a total expenditure of $250,000, Commissioner McCone presented the report to Governor Brown in the fanfare of television cameras on December 6.

"For what appears to have been political considerations connected with possible repercussions of the Watts affair on the 1966 gubernatorial campaign, only 100 days were available for an analysis of the most destructive incidents of racial violence in American history." (Governor Brown with the children of Watts.)

In view of the conditions under which it was hurried into existence, it should be no surprise that *Violence in the City—An End or a Beginning?* is a slim volume with only eighty-six pages of blown-up type. But the report of the McCone Commission is not only brief, it is sketchy and superficial. Its tone and style are disturbing. There is much glib writing and the approach as well as the format is slick in the manner of our illustrated news weeklies before their recent upgrading. The depth analysis of this fateful outbreak can be read by an average reader in less than an hour —allowing ample time for contemplating the many photographs, both color and black-and-white.

A comparison with the careful and considered report of the Illinois' Governor's Commission which analyzed the 1919 Chicago race riots in a 672-page book *(The Negro in Chicago)* that required three years of planning, research, and writing to produce may well be unfair. But with the considerable budget and the academic sophistication available today, more was to be expected than the public relations statement presently in our hands.

It is not only the size and style of the McCone document that are disturbing. Its content is disappointing both in its omissions and in underlying political and philosophical perspectives. There is almost nothing in the report that is new or that gives consideration to the unique conditions of Los Angeles life and politics. As Los Angeles councilman Bill Mills commented, most of the material in the report documents conditions in the Negro ghetto that have been common knowledge to sociologists and the informed public for a generation.

More appalling are the report's deeper failures. With a narrow legalistic perspective that approached the riots in terms of the sanctity of law and order, the commissioners were unable (or unwilling) to read any social or political meaning into the August terror. There was no attempt to view the outbreak from the point of view of the Negro poor. The commissioners also play a dangerous game with the thorny problem of responsibility. The Negro community as a whole is absolved from responsibility for the rioting while local and national leaders (civil-rights moderates and extremists alike) are taken to task for inflaming mass dis-

"In a crude attempt at 'horse-trading' in the responsibility market, the positions of the Los Angeles police department and city administrators are consistently protected." (Commission chairman John A. McCone (left) and Los Angeles police chief, William H. Parker.)

content and undermining attachments to law and authority. (In his two-page dissenting comment appended to the main report, the Reverend James E. Jones, a Negro commissioner, criticizes the report for attempting "to put a lid on protest.")

In a crude attempt at "horse-trading" in the responsibility market, the positions of the Los Angeles police department and city administrators are consistently protected. In discounting the relevance of police provocation and city policies to the revolt without presenting any facts or evidence, the Commission not only protects powerful interests; it abdicates its mandate to seek out facts and establish as best as it could the objective reality. My most general and serious criticism of the report is this violation of its responsibility to seek truth and its frequent hiding behind opinion and hearsay.

CAUSES OF THE WATTS "REVOLT"

Lurking behind the Watts violence are three basic problems, according to the McCone Commission:

■ the widespread unemployment and "idleness" in the Negro ghetto;

■ the cultural and educational backwardness of black children that prevents the schools from preparing them for the labor market and integrating them into society.

■ the troubled state of police-community relations in the Negro neighborhoods.

EMPLOYMENT. The chapter on employment is forthright in its emphasis on jobs as a central problem and correct in its understanding that male dignity and family responsibility can hardly be expected when men are unable to find steady work. For example: "The most serious immediate problem that faces the Negro in our community is employment—securing and holding a job that provides him an opportunity for livelihood, a chance to earn the means to support himself, and his family, a dignity, and a reason to feel that he is a member of our community in a true and a very real sense." The Commission calls upon federal, state, and city government to create jobs for the Negro and Mexican-American poor. Corporations and labor unions are asked to end discrimination once and for all and to police their progress by keeping careful records on minority employment. Because the Commissioners are convinced that the majority of jobless Los Angeles Negroes are presently unemployable, they call for an expanded and better-coordinated program of job training; they wisely recommend that control of this effort be placed inside the Negro community.

These proposals on employment are worthwhile and necessary but they encourage a deceptive complacency. The report does not probe sufficiently into the depth and seriousness of the problem. There is no consideration of the impact of population trends and technological developments on the availability of jobs, especially for the unskilled, and no willingness to face the escalating employment needs in the rapid expansion of Los Angeles' Negro population. The report is irresponsible because its style and tone convey the impression that its relatively mild and moderate recommendations provide real solutions.

EDUCATION. The treatment of education is the one section of the McCone report that is based on a careful and first-hand study. Kenneth A. Martyn, professor of education at Los Angeles State College, investigated five areas within the Los Angeles City Unified School District as a

Commission consultant. Student achievement was compared for four "disadvantaged areas" (of which two were primarily Negro and close to the riot centers) and one "advantaged" area (predominantly white upper-middle class). Average student reading performances in the fifth, eighth, and eleventh grades reveal a consistent backwardness in the lower-class Negro and Mexican districts. The gap is most dramatic at the eighth grade, since by the eleventh many of the poorest "achievers" are already drop-outs. The average student in the white middle class area is in the 79th percentile in reading vocabulary based on national norms; the average students in "Negro" Watts and Avalon are in the 13th and 14th percentiles; the averages in the primarily Mexican areas of Boyle Heights and East Los Angeles are 16 and 17.

Martyn investigated the possibility of discrimination in educational facilities. Some inequalities were found, but hardly enough to explain the systematic backwardness of minority students. The Commission thus locates the problem of Negro school performance in what today is fashionably called "a culturally impoverished environment." Parents have little education and their own background does not foster an orientation toward achievement and learning. Crowded housing conditions are not favorable for disciplined study. And the precariousness of employment and the lack of models of achievement may further dull incentive. In order to break this pattern and "raise the scholastic achievement of the average Negro child up to or perhaps above the present average achievement level in the city," the Commission calls for an intensive infusion of educational resources into the Negro community focusing on three programs: pre-school learning on the model of "Headstart"; the reduction of class size; and the improvement of academic and behavioral counseling.

The McCone report accepts the conventional position that it is the "vicious circular" connection between education and employment that is the crux of the dilemma of the Negro poor. And it places its main bet on education and the future, rather than creating jobs to solve the problems of the present. If the achievement levels of present and future generations of Negro children can be sufficiently raised, they will be motivated to remain in the school system and assimilate the skills and training that will begin reversing this cyclical process. Unfortunately, the middle-class ethos which underlies the Commission's emphasis on future-orientation and achievement is irrelevant to the needs and outlook of the lower-class adult group whose problems of work and training are likely to intensify.

But even with a crash program in education, can the average poor Negro youth be motivated toward achievement and excellence when the condition of his people and community place him in a position of alienation and powerlessness *vis-a-vis* the larger society? What is missing in the report's analysis is a total picture of the Watts community as consistently deprived and disadvantaged in relation to Los Angeles as a whole. Fragmented hints of this picture abound in the report, particularly in the excellent discussion of the woefully inadequate transportation system, but the fragments are never pieced together. If they were, municipal officials would then have to bear some responsibility for permitting this systematic deprivation to persist. By singling out education as the strategic sphere for ameliorative efforts, the Commission aims its biggest guns on the target-area in which the city's hands are relatively "clean" and in which it is relatively easy to suggest that the cultural backgrounds and individual performances of *Negroes themselves* account for a good part of the problem.

THE POLICE ISSUE

If we don't get no good out of this, it will happen again. By good I mean an end to police harassment, and we need jobs. I got eight kids, and I've only worked 10 days this year. I ain't ever been a crook, but if they don't do something, I'm gonna have to *take* something. I don't know how they expect us to live. (Young man in "a striped shirt" quoted by Louise Meriwether, "What the People of Watts Say," *Frontier,* Oct. 1965.)

When a deprived segment of the population breaks out in a violent attack on society and its representatives, the *underlying* causes refer to those long-term elements in its situation that have produced its alienation and despair. *Immediate* causes refer to those more short-run irritants and grievances that have intensified feelings of anger and hatred and focussed them on specific targets. The immediate grievances and conditions that spark illegal violence must have the effect of weakening the oppressed group's normal disposition to accept, at least overtly, the authority structure and legal norms of the society—otherwise mass violence could not erupt. The young Watts Negro quoted above seems to be saying that from his standpoint "jobs" are the underlying cause, "police harassment" the immediate issue. The governor's commission disagrees with his analysis and has its own explanation for the ghetto's sudden loss of attachment to the legal order.

It answers its own question, "Why Los Angeles?" in a way that almost totally relieves the city and county of implication. The rapid migration of Southern Negroes to the city's ghetto serves as their starting point, for these Negroes are unrealistic in expecting that California living will solve all their life-problems. In the context of this "crisis of expectations" Negro frustration and despair were fanned by three "aggravating events in the twelve months prior to the riots":

■ "Publicity given to the glowing promise of the federal poverty program was paralleled by reports of controversy and bickering over the mechanism to handle the program here in Los Angeles, and when the projects did arrive, they did not live up to expectation."

■ "Throughout the nation, unpunished violence and disobedience to law were widely reported, and almost daily there were exhortations, here and elsewhere, to take the most extreme and even illegal remedies to right a wide variety of wrongs, *real and supposed.*"

■ "In addition, many Negroes here felt and *were encouraged to feel* that they had been affronted by the passage of Proposition 14—an initiative measure passed by two-thirds of the voters in November 1964 which repealed the Rumford Fair Housing Act and unless modified by the voters or invalidated by the courts will bar any attempt by state or local governments to enact similar laws." (Italics mine.)

"In discussing the businesses which were looted and burned the Commission concludes (unlike most informed observers) that there was 'no significant correlation between alleged consumer exploitation and the destruction.'"

The argument is clear. Aside from some blunderings over the anti-poverty war, it was Negro leadership that undermined the commitment of law-abiding black citizens to authority and legal methods of redressing their grievances. What is important is the assumption that the Negro poor's attachment to law and political authority was not weakened by its own experience with police and other official representatives of society, but was instead subverted by an extremist and opportunist leadership. Such an analysis gives the Commission a free field to discount the role of the Los Angeles police and their presence in the ghetto as immediate recipitants of the violence. In short, the Commission has "bought" the line of Chief of Police William Parker who has consistently argued that the riot was a revolt of the criminal and lawless element, prodded on by a Negro leadership which inflamed the Los Angeles black community with the "bugaboo" of "police brutality."

The report devotes a chapter to law enforcement and police-community relations. It takes note of the severe criticism of the police department by many Negro witnesses

and frankly admits "the deep and longstanding schism between a substantial portion of the Negro community and
the police department." Considering the virtual unanimity
in the Negro community concerning police practices as the
foremost immediate cause of the outbreak, why did not the
Commission seriously investigate the role of law enforcement in the ghetto? The Commission acknowledges that
Negro *feelings* of oppressive police action were significant
conditions of the rioting. However, it violates its responsibility to truth and impartiality by refusing to examine the
factual basis of Negro opinion while stating the beliefs and
hearsay of white officers in an aura of established truth:

> . . . the police have explained to us the extent to which
> the conduct of some Negroes when apprehended has re-
> quired the use of force in making arrests. Example after
> example has been recited of arrestees, both men and
> women, becoming violent, struggling to resist arrest.
> and thus requiring removal by physical force. Other
> actions, each provocative to the police and each requiring
> more than normal action by the police in order to make
> an arrest or to perform other duties, have been described
> to us.

Precisely the same line is taken with respect to Chief
Parker. The Commission duly notes that the outspoken
chief is a focal point of criticism and is distrusted by most
Negroes. They feel he hates them. Yet the report con-
veniently omits all rational and objective evidence for such
Negro "belief" based on a whole series of public statements
made long before the riots. The inference is that Negro
belief rests on misinterpretation of fact and paranoid re-
actions.

However, not only embittered Negro attitudes, but *facts*
exist about the police presence in the ghetto—if the Commission would have only looked for them. There was a
Youth Opportunities Board study available to the Commission based on intensive interviews with 220 people in
the Watts, Willowbrook, and Avalon districts undertaken
only two years before the outbreak in this very area. The
sample included 70 delinquent and nondelinquent children,
26 parents, and 124 high administrators and lesser per-

sonnel of the major agencies in the community (schools, welfare and probation, recreation and youth groups). Attitudes toward the critical agencies of the community were probed, and it was found that of all the "serving institutions" of the larger society greatest hostility was directed toward the police department. A majority of adults as well as children felt that *the behavior of police aggravated the problems of growing up in the Negro community rather than contributed to their solution;* this was in direct contrast to their attitudes toward the schools, the parks, the health services, and the probation officers.

The real issue has perhaps been muddied by the outcry against "police brutality," the term that Negroes use to sum up their felt sense of grievance against law-enforcement agents. The police liberalization policy of recent years may well have reduced the number of cases of "classic" brutality—beatings, cruel methods of questioning, etc. What the Negro community is presently complaining about when it cries "police brutality" is the more subtle attack on personal dignity that manifests itself in unexplainable questionings and searches, in hostile and insolent attitudes toward groups of young Negroes on the street, or in cars, and in the use of disrespectful and sometimes racist language—in short, what the Watts man quoted above called "police harassment." There is no evidence that this assault on individual self-esteem and dignity has ceased.

Another facet of police brutality is the use of excessive force to control criminal and illegal behavior. Characteristically the Commission passed on its opportunity (and obligation) to assess the use of force by the various law enforcement agencies that put down the August violence, despite its considerable attention to their logistical and coordination problems and the concern of Negroes and liberal groups like the ACLU with what appeared to be unnecessary shootings of looters, including young children.

The police chapter is primarily devoted to the adequacy of procedures presently available for processing complaints against officer misconduct and to recommendations for improving both them and the general relation between law enforcement and the Negro community. Yet, the demand of

Negro leaders and white liberals for an independent civilian review board is described as "clamor"; the proposal is rejected because this device would "endanger the effectiveness of law enforcement." Experience with its use in two cities "has not demonstrated" its "advantages," but characteristically no evidence is given and the cities are not even named. Instead the report advocates the strengthening of the authority of the present Board of Police Commissioners, the civilian heads of the department, and establishment of the new position of Inspector General under the authority of the Chief of Police. The latter "would be responsible for making investigations and recommendations on all citizen complaints." In addition, the police should improve its community relations programs in the ghetto areas and strive to attract more Negroes and Mexicans to careers in law-enforcement.

The Commissioners are aware that "police brutality" has been an issue in all of the Northern Negro riots in recent years and that each began with a police incident. But instead of asking why poor Negroes come to believe that law and authority are not *their* law and their authority, they go on to sermonize:

> Our society is held together by respect for law. A group of officers who represent a tiny fraction of one percent of the population is the thin thread that enforces observance of law by those few who would do otherwise. If police authority is destroyed, if their effectiveness is impaired, and if their determination to use the authority vested in them to preserve a law abiding community is frustrated, all of society will suffer because groups would feel free to disobey the law and inevitably their number would increase. Chaos might easily result.

CHARACTER OF THE WATTS OUTBREAK

There is very little explicit consideration of the character and meaning of the outburst in the McCone Report, in spite• of its great concern with causes. The Commission missed an important point of departure by not viewing the Watts violence as a problematic phenomenon, the essence of which needed to be determined through a careful weighing of evidence and through social and political analysis. For this reason the report's implicit assumptions must be inferred because they are introduced in passing and never clearly spelled out.

The analytical perspective is overwhelmingly *riot control* rather than collective or crowd behavior. The attempt of responsible Negro leaders to cool off the mobs is discussed,

". . . The police have explained to us (the McCone Commission) the extent to which the conduct of some Negroes when apprehended has required the use of force in making arrests." (Excerpt from the report.)

but the major emphasis is on the tactics used by the various law enforcement agencies. After a fairly thorough discussion of the arrest which set off the events, the Negroes who participated in violence are almost excluded from the story. The very language of the Commission suggests that it has prejudged "the meaning of Watts," even though the debate that has been going on in Negro circles as to the appropriate term of reference suggests that determining the character of these events is a real and difficult question.

On page one of the report, the outbreak is called a "spasm" and "an insensate rage of destruction." Later it is called "an explosion—a *formless, quite senseless, all but hopeless violent protest*" (Italics mine). Only in its discussion of the business targets which were looted and burned does the Commission attempt to locate a meaning or pattern in what the rioters did, and here they conclude—unlike most informed observers—that there was no "significant correlation between alleged consumer exploitation and the destruction."

The legalistic perspective of the Commission and its staff seems to have blocked its sensitivity to the sociological meaning of the riots. When viewed simply as an uprising of the criminal element against law and order (aggravated of course by the more social, economic, and political causes of frustration already discussed), the Commissioners need not look seriously at its human meaning nor need they understand what messages may have been communicated by the rocks, gunfire, and Molotov cocktails. Let us not romanticize the Watts violence. I don't claim that everyone involved and everything done had rational motives. But it is a more humble and scientific attitude to leave the question open and to examine the limited evidence that is available. For the assumption of meaninglessness, the emptying out of content and communication from any set of human actions—*even nonrational violence*—reduces the dignity of the actors involved. In the present context it is a subtle insult to Los Angeles' Negroes. The report ostensibly avoids such an insulting stance by minimizing Negro participation and exculpating the bulk of the community from responsibility from the anti-social outbreak—except of course its leaders who aggravated the underlying tension:

In the ugliest interval which lasted from Thursday through Saturday, perhaps as many as 10,000 Negroes took to the streets in marauding bands. . . . The entire Negro population of Los Angeles County, about two thirds of whom live in this area (that of the riots), numbers more than 650,000. Observers estimate that only about two percent were involved in the disorder. Nevertheless, this violent fraction, however, minor, has given the face of community relations in Los Angeles a sinister cast.

No evidence is presented for the 2 percent estimate, nor for the total of 10,000 participants on which it is based.

We are not told how the Commission defines being "involved in the disorder." A number of distortions are apparently obvious, however. Even if 10,000 were the upper limit, this figure would indicate much more than 2 percent participation. For the Negro curfew area of some 500,000 residents contains many neighborhoods of comfortable middle-class people who were far from the riot center; they should be eliminated from a calculation of the extent of participation in an outbreak of the Negro poor and dispossessed. Second, the total population figures include women, children, and the aged. A more appropriate (and still difficult) question would be the extent of participation of young and mature Negro males in the low-income districts that were the centers of the action.

THE SPIRIT OF REVOLT

Unfortunately, I cannot answer this question precisely, but in view of the Commission's unscientific methodology and dubious deductions there is no reason to accept their view of the participation issue. Consider on this matter Bayard Rustin, who visited Watts with Martin Luther King a few days after the outbreak:

> I could not count heads but reports I have received and my experience with the people leads me to believe that a large percentage of the people living in the Watts area participated. But most of them did not themselves loot and burn but they were on the streets at one time or other. (*New America,* September 17, 1965)

As Rustin suggests, the question is not simply how many engaged in lawless acts. Essential to the meaning of the revolt is the attitude of the "non-participants" toward those who erupted in hate and violence. In the most popular revolutions it is only a small minority that storms the Bastille or dumps tea in Boston Harbor. Only through considering the viewpoints of the "silent mass" is it possible to know whether the Watts riots represented an action of a large segment of Los Angeles Negro poor rather than a cutting loose of a small "violent fraction." Had the McCone Commission done its job, it would have conducted a systematic survey of community opinion to determine the distribution of sentiment in Negro Los Angeles.

My informants reported widespread support within the ghetto for the violent outbreak. Moral approval (as well as active participation) was stronger among youth and among the poor and working-class. Old people and middle-class Negroes were more likely to feel ambivalent and hold back. But there seems to have been at least some participation from all segments of the black community. In the countless interviews and feature stories that appeared in the press and on television, Watts Negroes were more likely to explain and justify the riots rather than to condemn them—certainly the mass media would have little interest in censoring accounts of Negro disapproval. In a statewide public opinion survey conducted in November only 16 percent of the Negroes interviewed attributed the riots to "lack of respect for law and order" in contrast to 36 percent of the whites; "outside agitators" were seen as a most important cause by a scant 7 percent of the Negroes compared to 28 percent of the whites. Seventy-nine percent of the Negro respondents fixed upon "widespread unemployment" and "bad living conditions" as prime causes, compared with only 37 percent of the whites. And months after the rioting a poll conducted by ABC Television found that the proportion of Watts residents who felt that the summer's events had helped the Negroes' cause was twice as much as those who felt it had hurt them.

If the Los Angeles revolt was not simply a "spasm" of lawlessness reflecting the violent inclinations of a minor criminal group, but represented instead the mood and spirit of the low-income Negro community—then we must look more closely at what the crowds were attempting to communicate in their assault upon society.

As the Governor's report correctly notes, the uprising was not organized in advance. Yet it was neither formless nor meaningless. The Negro crowds were expressing more than the blind rage and the anti-white hate epitomized in the "Burn, baby, burn" slogan. They seem to have been announcing an unwillingness to continue to accept indignity and frustration without fighting back. They were particularly communicating their hatred of policemen, firemen, and other representatives of white society who operate in the Negro community "like an army of occupation." They were asserting a claim to territoriality, an unorganized and rather inchoate attempt to gain control over their community, their "turf." Most of the actions of the rioters appear to have been informed by the desire to clear out an alien presence, white men, rather than to kill them. (People have remarked how few whites were shot considering the degree of sniping and the marksmanship evidenced in accurate hits on automobile lights and other targets.) It was primarily an attack on property, particularly white-owned businesses, and not persons. Why not listen to what people in the crowds were saying as did Charles Hillinger of the *Los Angeles Times* on the night of August 13:

■ "White devils, what are you doing in here?"

■ "It's too late, white man. You had your chance. Now it's our turn."

■ "You created this monster and it's going to consume you. White man, you got a tiger by the tail. You can't hold it. You can't let it go."

■ "White man, you started all this the day you brought the first slave to this country."

■ "That's the hate that hate produced, white man. This ain't hurting us now. We have nothing to lose. Negroes don't own the buildings. You never did a decent thing in your life for us, white man."

A "NATIVE" UPRISING

Any appraisal of the Watts uprising must be tentative. All the facts are not yet known, and it always takes time to assimilate the full significance of historic and traumatic events. I suggest, however, that it was not primarily a rising of the lawless, despite the high participation of the *lumpenproletariat* and the clearcut attack on law and authority. Neither was it a "conventional race riot" for the Los Angeles terror arose from the initiative of the Negro community and did not fit the simple pattern of whites and blacks engaging in purely racial aggression. And it was not a Los Angeles version of a mass civil rights protest. Its organization was too loose. More important, the guiding impulse was not integration with American society but an attempt to stake out a sphere of control by moving against that society.

Instead my interpretation turns on two points. On the *collective* level the revolt seems to represent the crystallization of community identity through a nationalistic outburst against a society felt as dominating and oppressive. The spirit of the Watts rioters appears similar to that of anticolonial crowds demonstrating against foreign masters, though in America of course the objective situation and potential power relations are very different. On the *individual* level, participation would seem to have had a special appeal for those young Negroes whose aspirations to be men of dignity are systematically negated by the unavailability of work and the humiliations experienced in contacts with whites. For these young men (and reports indicate that males between the ages of 14 and 30 predominated in the

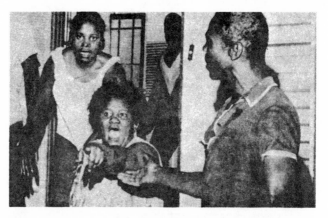

"The Negro crowds were expressing more than blind rage and anti-white hate; they seem to have been announcing an unwillingness to continue to accept indignity and frustration without fighting back."

streets), violence permitted expressing their manhood in the American way of fighting back and "getting even"—rather than the passive withdrawal which has been a more characteristic response of the Negro poor.

The gulf between Watts and affluent Los Angeles is disturbingly similar to the cleavage between the lives and interests of "natives" and their colonial masters. The poor Negro's alienation from the institutions and values of the larger society was made clear during the revolt. The sacredness of private property, that unconsciously accepted bulwark of our social arrangements, was rejected; Negroes who looted, apparently without guilt, generally remarked that they were taking things that "really belong" to them anyway. The society's bases of legitimacy and its loci of authority were attacked.

Thus Watts was not simply a racial uprising. Negro police and "responsible" moderate leaders were also the objects of the crowd's anger. Black businessmen who were seen as close to the Negro community were spared damage. From the standpoint of the poor, there was thus an implicit division of the Negro middle-class into those two segments that are found in the colonial situation: a "national bourgeoisie" on the side of liberation and a "native" middle-class that serves as agents for the dominant power arrangements.

Sartre has argued that colonialism reduced the manhood of the peoples it subjected in violating the integrity of indigenous ways of life and in creating the social status of "natives." The condition of slavery in the U.S. and the subsequent history of economic exploitation and second-class citizenship have constituted a similar attack on the manhood of Negro males. The chief contemporary manifestation of this crisis, according to the controversial "Moynihan report," is the precarious position of the man in the lower-class Negro family. The active dominance of the Negro woman and the male's relative passivity and instability are in part a residue of this historical process of manhood reduction; it is of course intimately reinforced by the unavailability of employment and the crisis of authority this brings about in the family. Unable to validate a sense of manly worth in terms of the larger cultural standards of economic responsibility, the lower-class youth orients himself toward the all-male street society whose manhood centers around other values and styles—hip, cool, and soul.

A new generation of Negro militants have created in the civil rights movement a vehicle for the affirmation of their manhood in the political struggle against its systematic negation. But the nonviolent movement which grew up in the South (with its more religiously oriented population, cohesive communities, and clear-cut segregation problems) is not well-adapted to the social condition and psychological temper of the Northern Negro. Unless new possibilities for the expression of initiative, assertiveness, and control are opened, we can expect that violent revolt will become increasingly frequent.

The Watts revolt was also a groping toward community identity. South-central Los Angeles has been a vast Negro ghetto with very amorphous neighborhood and district boundaries, with a glaring lack of leadership and organization. Most of the major civil rights groups were non-existent in the ghetto; the gap between official Negro spokesman and the poor was even greater than is typical. The word "Watts" itself as a locational reference for the ambiguously-defined district around 103rd and Central had become a stigmatized term among Negroes as well as whites and was rarely used by residents. During the August uprising a reversal in all these tendencies became apparent. The mass action strengthened feeble communal loyalties. The term "Watts" appeared painted on walls and windows as an expression of pride and identity. Youth gangs representing the adjacent neighborhoods of Watts, Willowbrook, and Compton ceased their long standing wars and united to provide a core of organization during the rioting and the subsequent rehabilitation work. Many middle-class blacks saw that their interests could not be severed from those of the ghetto's poor, particularly when their streets and residences were placed within the curfew boundaries drawn by the militia—thus dramatizing the fact of common fate. And since August, a proliferation of community organizing, political action, and civil rights groups have risen up in the Watts area. All these processes—intensified communal bonds, ethnic identity, the hesitant return of the middle-class, and a new sense of pride in place—are graphically summed up in the experience of Stan Saunders, a Watts boy who had moved out of the ghetto to All-American football honors at Whittier College and two years abroad as a Rhodes scholar. His return to Watts two weeks before the revolt may be prototypical:

At the height of the violence, he found himself joyously speaking the nitty-gritty Negro argot he hadn't used since junior high school, and despite the horrors of the night, this morning he felt a strange pride in Watts. As a riot, he told me, "It was a masterful performance. I sense a change there now, a buzz, and it tickles. For the first time people in Watts feel a pride in being black. I remember, when I first went to Whittier, I worried that if I didn't make it there, if I was rejected, I wouldn't have a place to go back to. Now I can say "I'm from Watts." (LIFE, August 27, 1965)

The McCone Commission missed the meaning of the Watts revolt due to the limitations inherent in its perspective. The surface radicalism of its language (in calling for "a new and, we believe, revolutionary attitude toward the problems of the city") cannot belie its basic status-quo orientation. The report advocates "costly and extreme recommendations," and while many of their excellent proposals are indeed costly, they are by no means extreme.

Truly effective proposals would hurt those established institutions and interests that gain from the deprivation of Watts and similar communities—the Commission does not fish in troubled waters. Possibly because they do not want Negroes to control their ethnic neighborhoods, they do not see the relation between community powerlessness and the generalized frustration and alienation which alarms them.

In their approach to the integration of the alienated Negro poor into American society, the Commission is guided by values and assumptions of the white middle-class ethos which are of dubious relevance to the majority of lower-class blacks. Their chief hope for the future is the instillation of achievement motivation in the ghetto poor so that they might embark upon the educational and occupational careers that exemplify the American success story. I am not against middle-class values—but in the immediate critical period ahead "middle-classification" will be effective only with a minority of today's poor.

What is needed—in addition to jobs—is an experimental program for finding innovations that might link the values and social patterns of the Negro lower class with the social and productive needs of the greater society, thus reversing the trend toward alienation. Before the meaningful recommendations can be made that are in line with the enormity of the problem, the sociological and cultural character of the Negro low-income community must be understood. The legalistically-oriented Commission—with its primary commitments to control, law and order, a white-dominated *status quo,* and a middle-class ethic—has not been able to do this.

Robert Blauner, assistant professor of sociology at the University of California at Berkeley, wrote *Alienation and Freedom: The Factory Worker and His Industry* (University of Chicago Press, 1964). He is currently at work on a book tentatively entitled *The Unique Americans,* a study of Negroes and other American ethnic groups, with special emphasis on manhood. He was a consultant to the McCone Commission.

The author gratefully acknowledges the aid of Lloyd Street who oriented him to Los Angeles and its Negro community and provided many observations and insights on the Watts rioting.